This book belongs to:

_____

_____

ISBN 3-88117-368-4
5th printing 1998
© Copyright 1984 Verlag Wolfgang Hölker GmbH
Martinistrasse 2, 48143 Münster
Auslieferung Schweiz: Baumgartner Bücher
Binzstrasse 5, CH-8953 Dietikon-Zürich
Translation: Jaqueline Jeffers
Printed in Germany by Druckhaus Cramer, Greven

# Cooking in Switzerland

Collected, recorded and tested by

*Marianne Kaltenbach*

published by
Wolfgang Hölker

**Marianne Kaltenbach** is Swiss and the author of successful cookbooks; as gastronomic journalist she writes columns, recipe cards and articles for important magazines. Her extensive activities in this domain have brought her honours and recognition. So, among others, she was made a "Conseillère Gastronomique du Bailliage National Suisse de la Chaîne des Rôtisseurs", conducts the secretariat of the "Union Suisse des Journalistes Gastronomes" (FIPREGA), is Officer of the Club Prosper Montagné and Member of the Académie Suisse des Gastronomes. Various awards for her services include a first price of the Comité National du Grand Prix des Guides touristiques and silver medals for her different works as "Creative Cooking" and "Recipes from My Old Mill".

Four years ago Marianne Kaltenbach opened her own restaurant in Lucerne (Zum Raben), where her guests delight in her marvellous specialities.

Her very personal and clearly explained recipes, all tested in her own experimental kitchen, are immensely popular among all cook enthusiasts. They enable the most inexperienced to run a high standard kitchen. And — probably the best attestation of their intrinsic merit — the books of Marianne Kaltenbach are not tucked away in the bookcase after being read, but find their place in the kitchen.

# The Table of Contents

# Preface

Switzerland's cuisine is as varied as its landscape. The products used may differ considerably depending on whether you are in a mountainous area, on the shores of a lake or in a fertile valley. In the Alps, where the cows graze during the summer, the cowherds cook with what they have, namely milk, butter, cream and cheese. Our lakes and rivers have a growing and varied fish population, and fertile valleys and plains offer an abundance of fruits and vegetables. In many places the farmers are still self-sufficient. The slaughtering of a pig is always followed by a feast, and the fresh meat is served either plain or in the form of sausages. The larger cities were known for their unique cuisine as well, but over the years it has lost some of its originality. Nonetheless, here and there, traditions are still highly regarded.

Although the recipes can be more conveniently prepared than in the past, there is today a noticeable revival of the cuisine of our ancestors. Naturally it is necessary that we change with the times, but it is important that the good things in life, no matter how old, are cherished and not forgotten.

Foreigners who visit our country enjoy getting to know the genuine Swiss cuisine. They then gladly do without their well known international dishes, which are offered most anywhere in the course of a tour through the country. This book offers a selection of our most popular dishes. These recipes have outlived all fashion trends and they certainly do justice to our beautiful country.

I hope that you will enjoy trying out and becoming acquainted with our regional specialities. Perhaps one or two dishes will bring back pleasant memories of your last vacation in Switzerland . . .


"En Guete"*

*M. Kallenbach*

* Bon appetit!

HELVETIA,
cum finitimis
regionibus
confœderatis.

Burgundiæ
pars.

Genever fee

Sabaudiæ pars.

Befchribet
Gerard Mercator,
et excudebat
Guilielmus Blaeu.

## Aargau

Geographically, this canton is a fertile piece of midland, with a cuisine best known for its fruit and vegetable dishes. Popular specialities include "Kartoffelpfluten" (potato dumplings drenched with butter), the unbelievably good "Rüeblitorte", a carrot cake which still tastes delicious after several days, and "Chräbeli", an anise pastry traditionally served at Christmastime. Chräbeli however call for an experienced cook, because they have to be just the right shape.

The canton of Aargau reaches as far as the Rhine river, where fish is a favorite. Every year in August, in the city of Rheinfelden, the Fishermen's Guild has a cookout under the trees surrounding a citadel built on a small island in the Rhine. Everyone, grownups and children alike, are then welcome to feast on the fish of the Rhine prepared by members of the guild.

## Appenzell

Appenzell is dairy country. This is where the famous Appenzeller cheese comes from. It is thus not surprising that Appenzell prides itself in its excellent cheese specialities such as the original "Chäshappech", a cheese batter spiralled through a funnel into hot fat. The Appenzell cuisine is as sharp as the tongues of the people who live there. Often teased for their shortness, the Appenzellers have developed a biting humor. This area is also famous for its "Mostbröckli" (dried beef) and sweet specialities like flatcakes ("Rahmfladen") filled with cream or honey. As small as this canton is, it is certainly capable of defending and protecting its regional specialities and folklore.

## Basle

Ever since the Middle Ages, Basle has been a rich and scholarly city. The Baslers can be described as worldly-minded gourmets who maintain the cuisine of the neighboring Alsace as well as their own. Their fanciest meat dish is the "Lummelbraten", a roast prepared from fillet of beef.

Basle is proud of its traditions. On New Year's Day, for example, relatives come visiting between 11 and 12 o'clock, and it is customary to serve a glass of "Hypokras", a spice wine which dates as far back as the Middle Ages. With the wine are served the famous "Basle Leckerli", invented at the beginning of the 15th century for the dignitaries of the Basle council, because ordinary Lebkuchen just weren't good enough for them. The citizens of Basle do not always insist on gourmet meals though, they are just as satisfied with simple cooking; and therefore, every year during the carnival period they happily feast on flour soup and "Ziiblewäje" (onion pie).

## Bern

The Emmen Valley, commonly known as "cheese country", is especially adamant concerning the preservation of its local cuisine. Many dishes which are now served all over Switzerland, originated here; like "Rösti", grated or finely sliced potatoes fried in hot fat, or the "Bernese Platter", which includes everything produced on a typical "Metzgete" (slaughter day), such as: smoked and pickled pork, shank, snout, ears and tails, blood- and liver sausages and boiled beef, served, depending on the season, on a bed of sauerkraut and fresh or dried beans. The "Bern Braid", made from a yeast dough, is a standard at every fancy meal or big breakfast.
The world famous meringues are nowhere as good as in this area.
Very little remains of the traditional kitchen of the city of Bern. The only outstanding speciality is the "Ziebelechüche", an onion pie served on the occasion of the onion market which takes place on the fourth Monday in November in the old town of Bern.

## Freiburg

In this canton, which serves as the border between the French and German speaking parts of Switzerland, traditions and regional specialities are consciously upheld. This canton has everything, from the best milk to the thickest cream, the sweetest butter, the tastiest cheese, the best ham and any other agricultural products. It is no wonder therefore, that every fall, the Freiburgers celebrate the "Benichon", a kind of Thanksgiving. The great wealth of this area is then displayed in the form of a copius meal. This feast, or Menü as it is called, is also served in restaurants, and represents a genuine cross-section of the culinary specialities of this region. It is an oppulent, culinary delight.

The specialities of this canton include the soft, rich Freiburger Vacherin cheese and the world famous Gruyère. The oldest fondue recipe stems from Freiburg — it is the only one which does not include wine.

## Geneva

The Genevois kitchen is no doubt influenced by the French. Nevertheless, the French influences are partially combined with a more rustic cuisine. The most delicate dish out of the Geneva repertoire is the "Omble Chevalier", a char from Lake Geneva served in a white wine and butter sauce. The cheese soufflé from this area is another showpiece, while the Genevois still argue with the Vaudois concerning the origin of the delicious cheese sticks known as "Malakoffs". The soup of the "Mother Royaume" is a historical remnant. It is served on the occasion of the "Escalade", an annual celebration in memory of an unsuccessful attack on the city in December of 1602 by the Savoyards. The trademark of the festivity is the "marmite", a large pot filled with hot soup, which, according to the legend, was poured over the heads of the enemy by a courageous woman (Mère Royaume) thereby saving the city.

## Glarus

The most well known export of this canton is the "Schabzieger". This is a tasty herb cheese formed into small sticks. It is used to season pasta or mixed with butter and served with potatoes boiled in their jackets. One recipe popular beyond the canton's border is a pie made from Pâte Brisée, spread half with plum jam and half with almond paste. The Glarus fruitcakes follow a close second.

## Graubünden

Graubünden is a very large canton with a hearty cuisine based on the local produce. It shows influences from the south and the Habsburg monarchy. Typical examples are the dumpling variations and similar specialities combined with vegetables and dried fruit. Other famous dishes include the barley soup cooked with smoked meat, the lamb and venison dishes and the Chur meat pie. The world famous "Engadine Nut Cake" is just one example of the art of the Engadine bakers, many of whom achieved great recognition in foreign countries as well. The all time favorite, however, is still the air-dried beef; this is a delicacy one must have at least tried.

## Lucerne

Lucerne is known for its country fare. A few country inns still serve home style dried cod, a lenten fare from the Middle Ages when it was mainly a monestary repast. In contrast to the hearty country dishes, the city of Lucerne had a more delicate cuisine of fish and fancy pastries; such as the traditional "Lözarner Chögelipastete", a large meat pastry, and in the sweets category, Lucerne Lebkuchen, prepared with pear concentrate.

## Neuchâtel

The simplest fondue recipe stems from Neuchâtel. It is prepared with Gruyère, Emmentaler or spicy Jura cheese and local wine. This recipe serves as the basis for all other fondue variations in western Switzerland.

## St. Gallen

St. Gallen has always had very close ties with its monastery. Many of today's specialities were created by the monks, such as the St. Gallen monastery cake, which is slightly reminiscent of the Austrian "Linzer Torte". In St. Gallen's Rhine valley and around the Toggenburg area one can still find many country specialities prepared according to the old recipes.

13

## Schaffhausen

In the area around Schaffhausen, the people are especially fond of the fish from the Rhine river. Unfortunately these fish are becoming increasingly scarce. Favorites include grayling fried in plenty of butter and pike, sliced and deep-fried. The "Schübling", a large spicy sausage, is popular all over Switzerland. The "Schaffhauser Katzenzüngli" (cat tongues) can be bought in any local pastry shop. They are very delicate and brittle and therefore rather difficult to make yourself.

## Schwyz

In Schwyz, one of the oldest cantons of the Swiss confederation, milk, cream and cheese are the basis of every recipe. Here you will find delicious cheesecakes, hearty soups and healthy stews. Potatoes, called "Gummeli", are almost omnipresent. "Suuri Gummeli" is a popular speciality made from potato slices with a white, slightly sour sauce. On holidays, these "sour potatoes" are served as an accompaniement to "Suubäggli", a baked ham.

## Solothurn

Solothurn's kitchen does not have any particularly outstanding characteristics. A common dish is onions on bread with various sauces, called "Krausi". The "suure Mocke" (Sauerbraten) is Solothurn's only real speciality, but it is served in most other regions of German speaking Switzerland as well. "Güggeli (chicken) à l'Ambassador" is a last reminder of the city's days of glory.

## Ticino

The original Ticino cuisine is very simple and sparce. The people in the valleys had very few natural resources at their disposal, and they were much too poor to afford anything special. Genuine Ticino fare is found in the small restaurants in the Ticino valleys, where there are usually only about three tables for guests. Here you get exactly what is cooked for the family. In the grottos, where local wine is served, the menu will most likely only include chicken, a "stufato" (roast) or a few marinated fish. The Ticino kitchen of today is strongly influenced by the Italian cuisine from the Piemont and Lombardy regions. Polenta is still well liked, but unfortunately often forgotten. The preparation of polenta originates from an old Italian tradition. In the past, it was cooked over the fireplace or over charcoal in a copper kettle and stirred for 40 minutes in one direction. Other typical dishes, also inspired by the Italians, include the hearty minestrone in its many variations, the vegetable soups; especially the "Busecca" (with tripe), the "Manzo brasato", a beef roast with a rich red wine sauce, the "Osso bucco" (calves' knuckles) and, last but not least, the well known "Risotto". In the Maggia valley, risotto is prepared with dried mushrooms, giving it an especially unique flavour. Risotto is always served during the Ticino carnival. It is served in the street to the local population and the tourists; what was originally a free meal for the poor has over the years turned into a public festival.

## Thurgau

This canton is known for its abundant fruit trees and consequently for its fruit juice. Many dishes in this area include the various juices. Lake Constance offers a multitude of fish which are uniquely prepared. Wild coot, hunted in early winter, are a popular speciality. "Gottlieber Hüppen", delicate pastry rolls, stem from Gottlieben, a charming town on the lake near Constance.

## Unterwalden

This canton is divided into Ob-(upper) and Nid(lower)walden. It is characterized by a simple, frugal kitchen, with many unique specialities. Obwalden has a hearty mountain cuisine. Its most popular speciality is a noodle dish called "Ländermagronen". It is made with straight, hollow noodles (makkaroni) cooked in milk, mixed with diced potatoes and baked with a cover of cheese. It is served garnished with browned onions.

15

## Uri

Although the canton of Uri has a relatively barren landscape, its cuisine is probably the most interesting of central Switzerland. It demonstrates definite southern influences and it is thus not unusual to find chestnuts, rice, garlic and sharp spices in their recipes. Many dishes were inspired by looking over the shoulders of Italian workers, participating in the construction of the St. Gotthard tunnel. An especially tasty example is "Rys and Pohr", a type of risotto with leek (called porro in Italian) garnished with browned onions.
The most famous dishes of this area include the "Urner Häfelichabis", a spicy lamb and cabbage stew, and the "Älplermagronen", similar to the Ländermagronen from Obwalden, but without potatoes. The Uri cuisine also prides itself in excellent desserts made with dried fruit, like the "Brischtner Birä".

## Valais

Next to the Emmental cuisine, the Valaisian is surely one of the most popular in Switzerland. It owes its popularity to its abundance of vegetables and fruit which it delivers throughout Switzerland. They include asparagus, tomatoes, strawberries, apricots, grapes, apples, pears and cauliflower. The Valais has also made itself a name with its "Raclette" and dried raw ham, both of which are enjoyed in other parts of Switzerland with an appropriate Valais wine.

## Vaud

The widespread popularity of this region's cuisine, especially in the German speaking part of Switzerland, is largely due to its first-class white wines. The Vaudois recipes are totally in tune with the local wines. What would the saucissons, the saucisses au foie or aux choux or any of this region's sausage specialities be without a glass of St. Saphorin. A dry wine from this area is a perfect complement to cheese such as the various types of fondue or the cheese sticks known as "Malakoffs", which owe their names to the Vaudois mercenaries who brought the recipe back from Russia. In the spring one

16

serves delicious salads prepared with walnut oil. The pressed walnuts are also used in the unique "Gâteau aux nillons" with its dark, rich topping.

## Zug

Many gourmets travel to Zug solely for the tender "Röteli", a fish from the char family with reddish meat. They are only caught in November and are inimitably prepared: braised with herbs and white wine or boiled and served with melted butter. The second attraction of this lovely city along the lake of Zug is a cherry pie made from a biscuit dough soaked with kirsch and filled with a butter cream. This speciality is also popular beyond the city's borders. Aside from the above mentioned Röteli the restaurants do serve other fish from the lake such as whitefish and pike.

## Zurich

Zurich has more meat specialities than any other canton. The many beautiful guildhalls with their richly decorated rooms are remnants of the feasts and celebrations of the past. One of the oldest and noblest of meat dishes is called the "Spanish Soup". It was brought to Zurich from the courts of Europe and served in beautiful bronze bowls, which today can be admired in the Swiss National Museum. But there are so many other delicious specialities such as the tender "Leberspiessli" (liver kebabs with sage leaves) or the famous "Zürcher Geschnetzeltes", thinly sliced veal served in a wine sauce, sometimes mixed with veal kidneys and Rösti. Every visitor to Zurich is likely to be offered this speciality. Zurich's pastries date back to the Middle Ages. The "Zürcher Tirggeli", however, look better than they taste. They are made out of a honey/flour dough and formed into replicas of Zurich's objects of interest. The oldest of these dough models have long since become collectors' items. The preparation of chocolate in Zurich also has a respectable past. Chocolate milk already was a fashionable drink in the late 17th century. It was followed by the production of chocolate bits and whole bars of chocolate. The chocolate truffels, prepared daily, are the culmination of Zurich's "chocolate art". They are sold only by the best pastry shops and delivered all over the world.

17

fig. 2

# Soups and Stews

## a) Soups

Swiss soup specialities are hearty and nutritious. In the olden days, along with home-made bread, they served as the main meal of the day in the country and mountain regions. Today they are served with sausages or cheese and fruit for dessert.

## Basle Flour Soup

This is the traditional soup of the Basle carnival. It is served in the early morning hours after the "Morgenstraich" (the official opening of the Basle carnival) and again after everyone is tired and hungry from the "Gässle" (when the small, masked groups parade through the streets of Basle).

*2 Tbs butter, 4 Tbs flour, 1.2 L (1.2 qts) bouillon,*
*50 g (2 oz) grated cheese*

Melt the butter, add 2 Tbs flour and brown lightly, stirring constantly. Add the remaining flour, stir into the browned flour and remove pan from heat. Pour in bouillon and stir well. Be sure not to let it get lumpy. Simmer at low heat for a minimum of 45 minutes, stirring occasionally. Serve in soup bowls and top with grated cheese.
Note: As desired, sprinkle with onion rings, croutons, chopped parsley or chives.

# Barley Soup

This barley soup is probably Graubünden's most popular speciality. It is so well liked that it is prepared in many other cantons as well.

## 6-8 servings

*2 carrots, 100 g (3½ oz) celery root, 2 large potatoes, 2 leeks, 2 celery leaves, 4-5 savoy cabbage leaves, ½ calf's foot, 1 Tbs butter, 100 g (3½ oz) barley, 2 L (2 qts) bouillon, salt, pepper, 1 onion, 1 bay leaf, 1 clove, 100 g (3½ oz) smoked lean bacon, 300 g (10½ oz) smoked pork, 200 g (7 oz) smoked beef, 1 egg yolk, 1 dl (⅓ C) cream*

Peel and dice the carrots, celery and potatoes. Cut the leek, celery and cabbage leaves into fine strips. Sauté the vegetables and calf's foot in the butter. Add the barley. After a few minutes pour in the bouillon. Stick the onion with the clove and add to the soup along with the bacon, pork and beef. Simmer for 2½ hours.

Remove the meat, calf's foot and onion from the soup. Dice the meat (separate the calf's foot from the bone) and return to the soup. Mix the egg with the cream and add to the soup. Heat, but do not boil. Season to taste with salt and pepper.

Note: If the soup is not meant as a stew, it's enough if you just add a piece of bacon rind instead of the meat and calf's foot. The egg and cream could also be left out, or use sausages instead of meat.


# Busecca
## (Ticino Tripe Soup)

A very old Ticino speciality. It's even more authentic if cooked with innards instead of tripe.

*1 onion, 2 garlic cloves, 100 g (3½ oz) diced bacon, 1 Tbs olive oil, 3 potatoes, 3 carrots, ½ celery root, 3 tomatoes, 2 leeks, 350 g (12 oz) pre-cooked tripe, salt, pepper, 1 dash saffron, marjoram, thyme, basil, rosemary, 2 Tbs tomato purée, 1 L (1 qt) bouillon, 3 Tbs grated cheese*

Chop the onions and press the garlic. Fry in hot oil with the bacon. Dice the carrots, potatoes, celery and tomatoes. Cut the leek into little wheels. Cut the tripe into strips and sauté with the vegetables. Season with salt and pepper as well as saffron, thyme, rosemary, basil and marjoram. Add the tomato purée and steam for 1-2 minutes. Bring to a boil and reduce heat. Cover and simmer gently for 30-40 minutes. Serve with grated cheese.

## Choscht Soup

In the mountain regions of Zurich, where the farmers lived a very frugal life, this was the daily main meal.

> *100 g (3¹/₂ oz) white beans, 100 g (3¹/₂ oz) barley, approx. 1 L (1 qt) bouillon, 150 g (5¹/₄ oz) lean diced bacon, 1 onion, 1 leek, 1 celery root, 2-3 potatoes, 1 Tbs butter, salt, pepper, savory*

Soak the beans and barley overnight in luke warm water. The following day, add the bouillon, bringing the total liquid measure to 2 L (2 qts). Bring this mixture to a boil and cook for 1 hour. Meanwhile, chop the onions, cut the celery and carrots into wheels and dice the potatoes. Brown these vegetables with the bacon cubes, in hot butter. Add to the soup and simmer for another 30 minutes. Season with salt, pepper and savory.
Note: You may enhance the soup by adding sausages (wieners or frankfurters) shortly before serving. Instead of beans try lentils or peas.

## Bern Pea Soup

> *500 g (2¹/₂ C) yellow peas, 100 g (3¹/₂ oz) diced bacon, 1 onion, 1 leek, 1 carrot, 1 small celery root, 4 slices bread, 2 Tbs butter*

Soak the peas overnight in 2 L (2 qts) water. In a deep saucepan, lightly brown the bacon. Clean the vegetables and chop into small pieces. Add to the bacon and steam briefly. Add the peas along with the liquid and simmer gently for 1¹/₂-2 hours. Season with salt and pepper. Cut the bread into small cubes and roast in butter shortly before serving. Serve these croutons either over the soup or in a separate dish.

Note: You can turn this soup into a delicious stew if you cook it with salted pig's knuckles.

In the Emmen Valley, after a slaughter, the soup is enhanced with the pig's snout, ears and tail.

## Emmental Potato Soup

### 6 servings

*1 onion, 2 Tbs butter, 1 kg (2.2 lbs) potatoes, 2 leeks, 2 carrots, 1½ L (1½ qts) bouillon, 1 tsp flour, 3-4 Tbs cream, 1 Tbs freshly chopped marjoram, 2 Tbs chopped parsley, salt, pepper, nutmeg, 1 tsp vinegar*

Chop the onions and brown them lightly in butter. Peel and dice the potatoes. Cut the leek into little wheels and the peeled carrots into small pieces. Add these vegetables to the onions. Sauté briefly, then pour in the bouillon. Simmer gently for 30 minutes. Remove the mixture from the saucepan and pass through a strainer. Return to saucepan. Mix the flour with the cream and add to the soup, followed by the parsley and marjoram. Simmer for another 10 minutes, stirring occasionally. Season to taste with salt, pepper and nutmeg. Stir in the vinegar shortly before serving.

Serve with croutons or place thin slices of Emmentaler cheese in the soup bowls and cover these with hot soup.

Note: The shot of vinegar adds that special touch to this soup — don't leave it out!

## Minestrone
## (Ticino Vegetable Soup)

*50 g (1³/₄ oz) kidney beans, 2 carrots, 1 leek, 1 piece celery root, 2 onions, 50 g (1³/₄ oz) diced bacon, 4 Tbs olive oil, 2 garlic cloves, 1¹/₂ L (1¹/₂ qts) bouillon, 2 Tbs chopped basil, 50 g (2 oz) rice or pasta, 50 g (2 oz) grated cheese*

Soak the beans overnight in cold water. Cut the carrots, leek and celery root into small pieces. Halve the onion and slice into fine strips. Heat the olive oil. Sauté the diced bacon until it becomes glassy. Add the vegetables, the drained beans and the pressed garlic cloves. Pour in the bouillon. Add the basil and simmer for 1 hour. In the last 10-20 minutes add the rice or pasta. Serve and sprinkle with grated cheese.

Note: You may also simply use a pork rind which is removed before serving, instead of the cracklings. Or, you can cook a piece of beef in the soup. In place of pasta or rice, one may use 1-2 diced potatoes. Depending on the season a variety of other vegetables may be added, eg. zucchini, tomatoes, cabbage, beans etc. It is well worth it to prepare double the given amount and freeze half of it. If you add more of each ingredient and serve the soup with fresh bread, it can be served as a main meal. Lukewarm and without rice or pasta, Minestrone is an ideal summer appetizer.

*Grandma's recipe*

## Lötsch Valley Lentil Soup

*220 g (1 C) lentils, 1 carrot, 1 leek, 1 onion, 1 Tbs butter, 1 piece (about 400 g / 14 oz) smoked pork (eg. lean bacon), 3-4 potatoes, salt, pepper, 1-2 dl (¹/₃-³/₄ C) white wine, ¹/₂ tsp chopped savory, 2 Tbs chopped parsley*

Soak the lentils overnight. Cut the carrot, leek and onion into small pieces and sauté in butter. Pour in the lentils together with the liquid. Add the pork and the diced potatoes. Cover and simmer gently for 1¹/₂-2 hours. Put the soup through a sieve or strainer. Return to saucepan, add wine and season to taste with salt and pepper. Cut the meat into small chunks and add to the soup along with the savory. Serve topped with parsley.

Note: Served with croutons (separately or sprinkled over the soup) this makes a filling meal.

## Cheese Soup

This nutritious meal is more than just a soup; it is normally served as a main dish. It is found in many variations not only in central Switzerland but also in the mountain regions, such as Graubünden and the Valais.

*300 g (10½ oz) bread (at least 3 days old), 450 g (1 lb) cheese, eg. 300 g (10½ oz) Gruyère and 100 g (3½ oz) Emmentaler, 1 L (1 qt) milk, salt, pepper, nutmeg, 2 onions, 3 Tbs butter*

Cut bread and cheese into thin slices and place in layers into a deep dish. Scald the milk, season with salt, pepper and nutmeg and pour into the dish. Let stand, covered overnight. Shortly before serving, pour mixture into a deep saucepan and bring to a boil. Stir carefully so that the bread does not fall apart. In a separate saucepan, sauté the chopped onions in butter until translucent. Serve soup topped with the sautéed onions.

Note: White bread will give the soup a smooth, delicate taste, whereas brown bread adds a more distinct flavor.

25

## b) Stews

The stew is actually a further development of soup. In the old days, one usually had only one heat source: either in the fireplace or over a wood stove. Therefore all the ingredients for a meal were put in one pot. Switzerland still has many such dishes, and every canton more or less has its own stew speciality. The most original recipes are found in this chapter.

## Cazzuola
### (Pork and Vegetable Stew)

*800 g (1½ lbs) salted pork, 1 leek, 1 small head cabbage, 1 celery stalk or 1 piece celery root, 2 carrots, 2 Tbs butter, 1 onion, 2 garlic cloves, 2½ dl (1 C) red wine, 2 dl (¾ C) bouillon, salt, pepper, 4 potatoes*

Soak the meat in cold water for a few hours in order to draw some of the salt. Cut the leek into swirls. Halve the cabbage and remove the hard core. Cut the cabbage into 2 cm (¾ in) wide strips. Remove the meat from the water and pat dry with a paper towel. Sauté in butter. Add the coarsly chopped onion and the pressed garlic cloves. Sauté briefly and add the wine. Add the vegetables. Season with salt and pepper and gradually pour in the bouillon. In the last 30 minutes, add the diced potatoes.
Note: The potatoes will acquire a slightly strange coloring due to the red wine. If you wish to avoid this, use white wine; although this will take away some of the substance.

## Lettuce à la Neuenburg

*4 small heads bibb lettuce, 1 L (1 qt) bouillon, 150 g (5 oz) lean bacon cubes, 1 Tbs butter, 1 onion, salt, pepper, 1 tongue sausage*

Wash the lettuce and remove the outer leaves. Cut the heads in half, lengthwise. Bring the bouillon to a boil and add the lettuce. Simmer for 10 minutes. Remove lettuce and drain. Grease an oven-proof dish with a bit of the butter. Fold the lettuce halves back together and arrange them side by side in the dish. Sauté the bacon in the remaining butter together with the chopped onion and pour over the lettuce. Add a bit of bouillon and bake in a preheated 200° C (390° F) oven for approx. 30 minutes.

The lettuce may acquire a bit of color but don't let it get too dark. You may want to use aluminum foil as a cover.

Meanwhile, let the sausages draw in hot water for 30 minutes. Cut into diagonal 1½ cm (½ in) thick slices and arrange over the lettuce.

## Plain in Pigna

This is a dish that the Graubündner housewives stick in the oven before going to church on Sundays.

> *1 kg (2.2 lbs) potatoes, 100 g (3½ oz) lean bacon, 150 g (5 oz) salami, 1 Tbs corn flour, 2 Tbs corn semolina, 3 Tbs raisins (as desired), 50 g (2 oz) thin slices lean bacon, 50 g (4 Tbs) butter, 2 dl (¾ C) milk, salt, pepper nutmeg, 2 Tbs butter flakes*

Peel and grate the raw potatoes. Dice the bacon and salami and mix together with the corn flour, corn semolina and raisins. Place in a baking dish and cover with the potato mixture. Melt the butter and stir into the milk. Season with salt, pepper and nutmeg and pour over the potatoes. Dot with butter. Bake in a 190° C (375° F) preheated oven for 1 hour. If the potatoes get too dark, cover then with a sheet of aluminum foil.

# Papet Vaudois
## (Leek Stew)

For this dish you actually need real Vaud sausages and the spicy Saucisse au foie, but one can use pork sausages instead.

### 4-6 servings

*1 kg (2.2 lbs) leek, 1 onion, 1 Tbs butter, 1 dl (¹/₃ C) white wine, 1-2 dl (¹/₃-³/₄ C) bouillon, 4-6 potatoes, 2-3 sausages, salt, pepper*

Cut the cleaned leek into 3-4 cm (1-1½ in) long pieces and chop the onions. Sauté leek and onions in butter. Pour in the wine. Cover and simmer gently for 15 minutes. Meanwhile, peel and dice the potatoes. Place potatoes over the leek, season to taste with salt and pepper and add the bouillon. After about 10 minutes, add the sausages and let draw for 20 minutes. By then, all the liquid should have been absorbed and the potatoes should be very tender.
Remove the sausages before serving. Rinse under hot water and slice. Arrange over the leek. Serve in the pot.

*Delicious!*

## Sauerkraut

*1 kg (2.2 lbs) raw sauerkraut, butter, 1 bay leaf, 4-6 juniper berries, 2 garlic cloves, 2 halved calves' or pigs' feet, 800 g (2 lbs) smoked pork shoulder, ½ L (2 C) apple wine, 300 g (10½ oz) Pâte Brisée (see page 108), 1 egg*

Grease a deep, ovenproof dish with butter. Fill lightly with sauerkraut. Add bay leaf, juniper berries and pressed garlic cloves. Place the pigs' or calves' feet and the smoked pork on top. Pour over the apple wine. Roll out dough until 3 mm (¹/₁₀ in) thick. Brush the edges of the baking dish with egg white. Gently place the dough ever the dish, firmly pressing the outer edge onto the rim of the dish. Brush with the beaten egg yolk and bake in a 180° C (356° F) preheated oven for 2½ hours. About halfway through, cover the dough with a piece of aluminum foil.

# Schnitz and Drunder

This is a somewhat peculiar dish which mixes sweet and sour. There are many different varieties of it. Often, fresh caramelized pears are used, depending on the region. In Lucerne it is called "Schnitz und Härdöpfel". Sometimes the bacon is left out; in that case it is served as an accompaniment.

> *250 g (9 oz) dried sweet apple slices, 100 g (3½ oz) dried pears, 100 g (½ C) sugar, 20 g (2 Tbs) butter, 750 g (1½ lbs) smoked lean bacon, 6 large potatoes, salt*

Rinse the fruit and soak in water overnight.
In a frying pan, lightly brown the sugar, stirring constantly. Add the drained fruit, turn frequently and pour in some of the soaking liquid. Place the bacon on top of the fruit. Peel and dice the potatoes and add to the fruit and bacon. Season with salt and cover. Simmer for 45 minutes at low heat.


# Schwynigs and Cheschtenä
# (Pork with Chestnuts)

> *400 g (14 oz) dried chestnuts, 800 g (1½ lbs) smoked pork, 50 g (¼ C) sugar, salt, pepper, 500 g (1 lb) potatoes*

Soak the chestnuts overnight in water. Boil the meat in water for 30-40 minutes. Remove all the brown skin from the chestnuts. Melt the sugar in a dry pan without stirring until caramelized and light brown in color. Remove from heat and pour in 1-2 dl (⅓-¾ C) meat stock. Return to heat and add the chestnuts. Season with salt and pepper and cover with the meat. Cover and gently simmer for 30 minutes. The chestnuts must not fall apart! In a seperate pan boil the peeled potatoes in lightly salted water.
Cut the meat into slices and arrange over the chestnuts. Serve with the potatoes.
Note: Often the potatoes are added to the meat and chestnuts 20 minutes before the end of the cooking time. In this case, sprinkle the potatoes lightly with salt.

## Urner Häfelichabis
## (Lamb and Cabbage Stew)

This is the most popular stew in central Switzerland and it comes in many variations. Lamb is always a basic ingredient, although it is sometimes mixed with pork.

*800 g (1½ lbs) lamb, 2 Tbs butter, 2 onions, 2 garlic cloves, 1 medium sized head cabbage, salt, pepper, 1 bay leaf, 2-3 dl (1 C) bouillon*

Cut the meat into 1½ inch cubes. Sauté in butter. Remove from saucepan. Halve the cabbage. Remove the hard core and the coarse outer leaves. Cut into strips 2 cm (½ in) wide. Chop the onions and sauté in the saucepan together with the cabbage. Add the pressed garlic clove. When the cabbage is limp, season with salt and pepper, add the bay leaf and return the meat to the pan. Pour in the bouillon and simmer lightly, covered, for 1½ hours. Meat and cabbage must be very tender. Before serving, season to taste with salt and pepper. Note: You may substitute half of the lamb with 400 g (14 oz) pork and replace 1 Tbs butter with 1 Tbs pork fat. In many regions it is customary to add diced potatoes in the last 30 minutes of cooking time.

## Cabbage Rolls

*1 head cabbage, salt, pepper, 2 day-old breakfast rolls, 1 dl (⅓ C) meat stock or milk, 1 onion, 1 Tbs parsley or chopped herbs as desired, 300 g (10½ oz) ground beef, 3 Tbs butter, 2 dl (¾ C) instant gravy*

Remove any damaged outer leaves. Carefully separate the large leaves from the core. Cut off the tough ribs. Boil the leaves for 10-15 minutes in a large pot of salted water. Remove one by one and place on a paper towel to dry. Meanwhile cut the rolls into small pieces and soak in meat stock or milk. Finely chop the onions and sauté in 1 Tbs butter with the herbs. Press the liquid out of the rolls and place in a bowl along with onions, herbs and meat. Mix well. Season generously with salt and pepper. Spoon this filling onto the cabbage leaves and carefully wrap the leaves around it. Secure with string or toothpicks. Sauté in the remaining butter. Pour in some gravy, cover and braise for 20-30 minutes.

Note: This dish is also delicious when prepared without meat. In this case, use an additional roll and mix the bread mixture with the finely chopped inner cabbage leaves. Mix in an egg as desired in order to hold the mass together. Instead of the gravy, you may use tomato sauce. This will also add a bit of extra color.

## Rispor
## (Rice and Leek)

A slightly "southern" dish from the canton of Uri.

> *800 g (1½ lbs) leek, 1 onion, 1 Tbs butter, 1 garlic clove, 1 L (1 qt) bouillon, 300 g (10½ oz) short-grain rice, salt, pepper, 100 g (3½ oz) grated cheese, 50 g (4 Tbs) fresh butter*

Clean the leek and cut into 1-2 cm (⅓-¾ in) long pieces. Chop the onions. Sauté onions and leek in butter. Add the pressed garlic clove. Pour in the bouillon and cook for 5 minutes. Add the rice, season with salt and pepper and reduce heat. Simmer over low heat for 18-20 minutes, stirring occasionally. As needed, add liquid from time to time, but by the end of the cooking time all the liquid should be absorbed. Before serving, stir in the grated cheese and butter. Serve immediately.

fig. 3

# Fish

Switzerland has numerous large and small lakes from which many different varieties of fish originate. The preparation of the fish is usually very simple. Mostly they are fried in butter or boiled in stock like "Blue Trout". Depending on the region, however, you will also find fish dishes with delicate sauces such as the "Zuger Röteli" or Geneva style char. In the area around the Rhine river, deep-fried fish are very popular, while further south, in the Ticino, one prefers large and small whitefish in various marinades.

## Grayling à la Schaffhausen

The grayling is a somewhat scarce fish with beautifully tender meat and a slight flavor of thyme. If you are lucky, you'll find it on the menu of good restaurants in the northeastern part of Switzerland. It tastes best braised in a generous amount of butter.

2 servings

*1 medium-sized grayling, salt, pepper, 2 Tbs flour, 50 g (4 Tbs) butter, juice of ½ lemon, butter for basting*

Draw the fish. Using a share knife, make five diagonal slices on both sides. Rub the fish inside and out with salt and pepper. Dust with flour and place in an ovenproof dish. Melt the butter in a small pan and trickle it over the fish. Bake in a moderate oven (150° C / 300° F) until golden brown. Baste frequently with butter. Remove from oven after 15-20 minutes and sprinkle with lemon juice and the remaining melted butter.

Note: You may follow the same recipe in preparing pike. A 1 kg (2.2 lbs) fish will suffice for 4 servings.

# Whitefish Thurgau Style

*4 medium-sized whitefish (approx. 220 g / 8 oz)
each, salt, pepper, 3 Tbs chopped, assorted herbs
(parsley, chervil, dill, taragon), juice of 1 lemon, 1 1/2 dl
(1/2 C) white wine, 50 g (4 Tbs) butter*

Pre-heat oven to 200° C (425° F).
Remove entrails and clean. Rub the fish inside and out with salt and
pepper. Place in a greased, ovenproof dish and sprinkle with the
herbs and lemon juice. Add the white wine and dot the fish with a
few flakes of butter. Cover the dish with aluminum foil and place in
the preheated oven. Braise for 10 minutes, then remove the tin foil
and spread fish with more butter. Bake for another 15-20 minutes.
Before serving, dot with the remaining butter.
Note: For a richer meal, roast 2-3 Tbs of almond slivers in a "dry"
(without butter) frying pan and sprinkle these over the fish before
serving.

# Coregoni in Carpione
# (Marinated Whitefish)

A fish dish you are sure to find in a Ticino grotto.

*4 small whitefish (about 180 g/6 oz), 1 Tbs flour,
4 Tbs olive oil, salt, pepper, 1 onion, 1 carrot, 1 leek,
1 piece celery root, 2 garlic cloves, 1 bay leaf, 2 cloves,
1 1/2 dl (1/2 C) white vinegar, 1 1/2 dl (1/2 C) white wine,
1 1/2 dl (1/2 C) bouillon, 2 Tbs chopped parsley*

Rub the cleaned fish inside and out with salt and pepper and coat
with flour. Sauté in 2 Tbs olive oil until golden brown and crisp.
Place the fish on a square platter. Cut the onions into strips, finely
dice the carrots and slice the leek. Sauté the vegetables and the
pressed garlic clove in the rest of the olive oil. Add the bay leaf and
douse with the vinegar, wine and bouillon. Season slightly with salt
and pour the lukewarm marinade over the fish. Let stand for at least
2-3 days. Garnish with parsley before serving.
Note: This dish is meant as an appetizer. If you wish to serve it as a
main meal, use larger fish of about 200-250 g (7-9 oz).

## Egli Fillets with Almonds
## (Perch)

*500-600 g (approx. 20 oz) perch, salt, pepper, 2 Tbs
lemon juice, 1 Tbs flour, 4 Tbs butter, 2 Tbs almond
slivers*

Sprinkle the fillets with salt, pepper and lemon juice. Let draw for
10 minutes. Melt 2 Tbs butter. Dust the fish lightly with flour and
sauté briefly in the butter. Place on a warm platter. Heat the remaining
butter and add the almonds. Sauté until golden brown. Pour, together
with the butter, over the fish and serve.

## Filets de Perches St. Saphorin
## (Perch Fillets)

This is a speciality which the people from the Lake Geneva region
prepare best. The sauce includes the same wine which will be served
with the meal, like, for example, the world famous Dézaley.

*600 g (21 oz) perch, salt, pepper, ½ Tbs freshly
chopped herbs (taragon, dill, parsley), 1 onion, 100 g
(3½ oz) fresh butter, ¼ L (1 C) white wine, 1 dl (⅓ C)
cream, 1 garlic clove*

Season the fillets with salt and pepper. Sprinkle with the herbs and
let stand for 1 hour. Finely chop the onions and briefly sauté in butter
over low heat. Pour in the white wine and add the fish. Simmer
gently, covered, for 10 minutes. Carefully remove the fish. Place on
a hot platter and cover. Allow the liquid in the pan to reduce by ½.
Add the cream and the pressed garlic clove and reduce a bit more.
Remove from heat. Add the remaining butter bit by bit, stirring
vigorously. Pour the sauce over the fish and serve immediately.

## Blue Trout with Butter

This is the classic Swiss fish dish. Of course fresh brook trout taste
the best, but nowadays unfortunately these are usually only caught
by hobby fishermen in small brooks or mountain lakes.

*4 fresh trout, salt, 1½-2 dl (½-¾ C) white vinegar, a
few peppercorns*

Clean the fish. Handle it as carefully as possible, so as not to disturb its natural coating of slime. This slime coating is what brings about the blue color. And remember, trout are not scaled!

Add salt, vinegar and pepper corns to 2 L (2 qts) water and bring to a boil. Reduce the heat. As soon as the water is no longer boiling, carefully plunge in the fish. The water must not boil again! Allow the fish to draw in this broth for 10-20 minutes depending upon their size. The fish is done when the fins can easily be pulled out.

Note: Serve immediately — either in the pan (if the fish was prepared in a special fish pan) or on a preheated platter. Serve with hot, melted butter (browned if you wish). Blue trout is traditionally accompanied by boiled potatoes.

## Friture du Lac
## (Deep-Fried Small Fish)

This can only be done with small fish because they are meant to be eaten with their heads and tails intact.

*800 g (1½ lbs) small, whole, sweet water fish, max.*
*10 cm (4 in) in length, 3 Tbs flour, salt, pepper, fat*
*for deep-frying, 1 lemon*

Pour the flour and a generous amount of salt and pepper (the fish will not absorb everything) into a paper bag. Add batches of fish and shake until they are completely coated. Remove the fish and fry in deep fat until golden brown. Place on a heated platter covered with a napkin. Cover with aluminum foil and keep warm. Proceed in the same manner with the remaining fish. Before serving, garnish the platter with lemon wedges.

## Char Geneva Style

This is an especially noble fish stemming from Switzerland's mountain lakes, but every once in a while it is found in Lake Geneva.

*4 scallions, 1 Tbs butter, 4 very fresh char (Ombles Chevalier), salt, pepper, 2 dl (3/4 C) white wine (if possible from the Lake Geneva area), 1 lemon*
*For the sauce: 2 Tbs butter, thyme and rosemary as desired, 1 egg yolk*

Sauté the scallions in butter until nearly tender. Rub the cleaned fish inside and out with a little salt and pepper and add to the onions. Pour in the wine until the fish are half covered. Sprinkle with lemon juice. Cover and braise in the hot stock for 20 minutes. Remove the fish and keep them where they will stay warm. Put the stock through a sieve or strainer. Melt the butter and flour in a small pan and add the strained fish stock. Season to taste with thyme, rosemary and salt. In a bowl, beat the egg yolk. Stir in some sauce, then add this mixture to the sauce. Reheat and scald. Pour over the fish. Serve with boiled potatoes.
Note: You may follow the same recipe in the preparation of trout.

## Char with Herbs

From the 15th of November to the 15th of December it is fishing season in Zug. Many gourmets make a special trip to Zug during this time in order to enjoy these delicate fish in one of the city's top restaurants.

*4 char, salt, pepper, 1 tsp flour, 1/2 Tbs butter, 1 onion, 2 Tbs chopped herbs (fresh, if possible), 2 dl (3/4 C) white wine, 2 dl (3/4 C) cream*

Rub the cleaned and drawn fish inside and out with salt and pepper. Dust very lightly with flour. Heat the butter in a saucepan and add the finely chopped onion and herbs. Sauté. Place the fish in the pan side by side and pour in the wine. Braise for 12-15 minutes, turning once. Carefully remove the fish and place on a warm platter. Bring the stock to a vigorous boil and reduce slightly. Add the cream and boil again. Season to taste with salt and pepper and pour over the fish.

# Deep-Fried Pike

Nowadays pike is primarily found in the areas surrounding the Rhine, Aare and Reuss rivers, where it is deep-fried.

*1 pike, approx. 1 kg (2.2 lbs), salt, pepper, juice of
1 lemon, 3 Tbs flour, fat for deep-frying, 2 lemons*

Cut the cleaned fish into 2 cm (¾ in) thick slices. Season on both sides with salt and pepper. Sprinkle with lemon juice and place on top of one another in a bowl. Let draw for 1 hour. Drain and dab dry with a paper towel. Dip first in the flour, then in the beaten eggs. Fry in deep fat heated to approx. 170° C (338° F) for 3-4 minutes. Drain and arrange on a platter covered with a napkin. Garnish with lemon wedges. Boiled potatoes with mayonnaise and salad are an especially good accomponiement.
If you like, you may bread the fish slices before deep-frying.

# Dried Cod

In the past it was customary in the Catholic regions of Switzerland, to eat dried cod on Good Friday. This saltwater fish was brought into central Switzerland via alpine passes such as the Gotthard Pass. Due to its durability it was very much in demand. The best recipes for this fish always came from the monestaries. Below is an old recipe from Lucerne which today is served as a speciality by certain families and a few restaurants.

4-6 servings

*1 kg (2.2 lbs) dried, salted cod, 2 dl (¾ C) milk, 2 bay
leaves, 2 cloves, 6 Tbs butter, pepper, 2 large onions*

Have the cod cut into pieces. Soak in cold water for 4-5 days (depending on salt content). Change the water daily.
Heat 1½ L (1½ qts) water with the milk, bay leaves and cloves. Add the fish pieces. Bring to a boil, reduce the heat and simmer covered, over low heat for 1½ hours. Drain the liquid and remove skin and bones from the fish. In a saucepan, heat 2 Tbs butter and add the fish. Sprinkle with pepper, cover and simmer for a few minutes. Melt the remaining butter in a separate pan and sauté the sliced onions. Arrange the onions over the prepared fish.

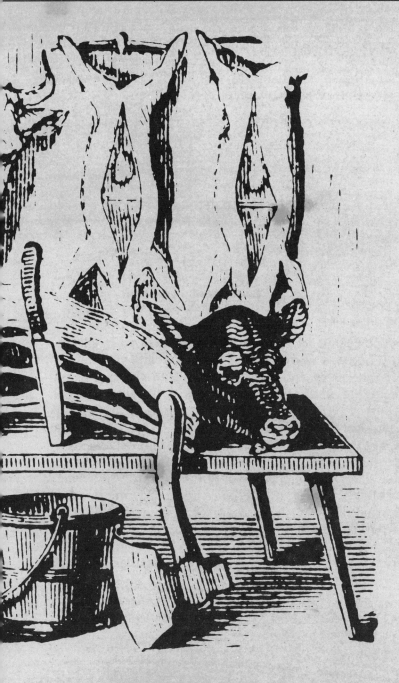

## a) Meat

In the old days in the country, if meat was served it was only on Sundays; and then usually only for the men. In the mountain cantons especially, this was a luxury that one could only seldom or never afford. In the cities and agricultural areas the situation was different. In the country pork predominated, especially on the occasion of a "Metzgete" (slaughter day). The city folk were more accustomed to the more delicate kinds of meat such as veal and beef. This chapter includes a cross-section of all Swiss meat specialities.

## Roasted Fillet of Beef

This is a typical city dish which in the olden days, only the aristocratic, rich citizens of Basle could afford. The Basle name for a fillet of beef is "Lummel".

> *1 kg (2.2 lbs) fillet of beef, larded with pork fat (have your butcher do it), 2 Tbs butter, salt, pepper, 1 carrot, 1 onion, 1 bay leaf, 1 clove, 1 small celery root, 1 dl ($^1/_3$ C) white wine, 3 Tbs cream, $^1/_2$ tsp cornstarch (as desired)*

Sauté the larded meat on all sides in butter. Season with salt and pepper. Peel and halve the carrot. Stick the onion with the bay leaf and clove. Peel the celery and add, together with the carrot and onion, to the meat. Steam briefly, then douse with the wine. Bake in a preheated 200° C (390° F) oven for 20-30 minutes, basting frequently. Control the heat with a meat thermometer. The meat should be pink, not well done. Remove the meat from the casserole, cover with aluminum foil and set in a warm place. Deglaze the juices with some water. Pour into a small saucepan and bring to a quick boil. Stir in cornstarch mixed with cream as desired. Bring to a boil again and simmer until the sauce is creamy. Slice the meat and place on a warm platter. Serve the sauce separately or poured over the meat.

Serve this festive dish with a variety of young vegetables and fried potatoes.

## Sauerbraten
## (Marinated Beef)

Sauerbraten is popular in many regions of Switzerland, but the taste is always unique because it is marinated in the local wine. Those that do not have their own wine add vinegar to the marinade and bind the sauce with sour cream.

*1 kg (2.2 lbs) beef chuck, eg. shoulder, ½ celery root, 1 leek, 2 carrots, 1 garlic clove, 1 clove, 6 juniper berries, 4 cardamom seeds, 4 coriander seeds, 12 pepper corns, thyme, 1 L (1 qt) red wine, 2 dl (¾ C) liquid instant gravy, 3 Tbs butter, 1 Tbs flour, salt, pepper, 2 Tbs sour cream, 1 piece dark bread (end piece)*

Dice half of the vegetables and cut have of the herbs into fine strips. Bring to a boil in 7 dl (2¾ C) wine. Place the meat in a deep bowl and pour over the hot marinade. Let stand in a cool place for 5 days. Be sure that the meat is always completely covered with wine.

After the 5 days have passed, remove the meat and pour out the marinade. Dab the meat dry with paper towelling. Sauté on all sides in 2 Tbs butter. Add the remaining chopped vegetables, herbs and bread. Let steam briefly, then pour in 3 dl (1¼ C) wine and simmer slowly for 2 hours. Add the dissolved instant gravy and reduce slightly. Knead the flour with the rest of the butter and stir into the sauce. Season with salt and pepper and enhance with sour cream. Simmer over low heat for 15 minutes.

Serve with mashed potatoes.

## Farmer Goulash

*600 g (21 oz) beef, cut into cubes, 2 Tbs butter, 50 g (2 oz) diced lean bacon, 1 onion, 1 leek, 3 carrots, 1 small celery root, 1 Tbs flour, salt, pepper, marjoram, ½ L (2 C) bouillon, 5 potatoes, 1 Tbs chopped parsley*

Sauté the meat pieces on all sides in butter. Add the bacon. Chop the onion and cut the leek diagonally. Dice the carrots and celery. Add vegetables and flour to the meat. Sprinkle with salt, pepper and mar-

43

joram and douse with the bouillon. Cover the pan and simmer either on the stove or in the oven, for 1½ hours. Add the diced potatoes and mix with the meat. Simmer 30 minutes longer. Serve garnished with parsley.

## Bernese Sauerkraut Platter

The story says that the Bernese Platter was created in the vicinity of Bern, when the victorious soldiers returned from a long battle. The women welcomed their men home by bringing everything they had in the house to a nearby inn where the food was cooked and eaten. Today's platter is made up of ham, bacon, sausages, beef, tongue, sauerkraut and beans.

### 6-8 servings

*1 onion, 1 Tbs pork fat, 1 kg (2.2 lbs) sauerkraut, 1 tsp juniper berries, 1 dl (¹/₃ C) white wine, 500 g (18 oz) smoked, lean bacon, 750 g (1½ lbs) smoked Kasseler (pork), 1 smoked beef tongue, 3-4 ham hocks, 1-2 pigs' ears or tails, 500 g (18 oz) beef for boiling, 500 g (18 oz) soup bones, 1 carrot, 1 piece celery root*

Sauté the chopped onion in pork fat until translucent. Press all liquid out of the sauerkraut and add to the onion together with the juniper berries. Let draw slightly, then douse with 3 dl (1¼ C) water. Place the bacon and Kasseler on top of the sauerkraut. Cover and cook for 1½ hours either on the stove or in the oven. Individual cooking time depends on the quality and size of the meat.

Place the tongue in a separate pot in unsalted water and let draw for 3-4 hours. In the last half, add the ham hocks and pigs' ears or tails. Boil the beef and soup bones in a separate pot as well.

Serve the meat stock first as desired. Cut the meat into slices. Place the drained sauerkraut on a platter and arrange the meat on top. Serve with boiled potatoes (peeled).

## Braised Lamb

Graubünden has a large free grazing sheep population. It is no wonder that many of the recipes date very far back. Here a typical recipe.

*800 g (1½ lbs) shoulder of lamb, 2 Tbs butter,*
*3 onions, 20 bay leaves, 1 garlic clove, ½ cinnamon*
*stick, salt, pepper, 3 dl (1¼ C) bouillon, 6 potatoes*

Cut the meat into chunks and sauté in the butter. Slice the onions and add to the meat. Sauté until they turn light brown. Add the bay leaves, salt, pepper, pressed garlic, cinnamon stick and bouillon. Cover the pot and simmer for 1½ hours. Peel the potatoes, cut into pieces and add to the meat. Simmer for another 30 minutes. Check frequently to make sure that their is enough liquid in the pot. There should be some stock left over at the end, so every once in a while pour in some bouillon.

## Lamb Roast

*800 g (1½ lbs) shoulder or neck of lamb, salt, pepper,*
*4 garlic cloves, 2 Tbs butter, 2 onions, 2 dl (¾ C) red*
*wine, 1 clove, 3 carrots, 1 small celery root, 500 g*
*(18 oz) potatoes, 1 sprig thyme, 2½ dl (1 C) bouillon*

Sprinkle the meat with pepper and stick with the halved garlic cloves. Sauté on all sides in hot butter. Sprinkle with salt and add the clove, onions and red wine. Cover and bake in a preheated 190° C (375° F) oven for 45-50 minutes. Peel carrots, celery root and potatoes. Cut into pieces and add, along with the sprig of thyme to the meat. Bake for another hour. Baste occasionally with bouillon.
When the meat is done, cut it into slices and serve in the pot, together with the vegetables and juices.
Note: This roast may also be prepared in an earthware lidded pot.

*My favorite*

# Gigot d'Agneau
## (Leg of Lamb)

This is a favorite meat dish in western Switzerland. It is a typical Easter recipe.

### 6-8 servings

*1 leg of lamb (about 1,3 kg/3 lbs), 2 garlic cloves,*
*3 Tbs butter, salt, pepper, 1 onion stuck with 1 clove*
*and 1 bay leaf, 3 dl (1¼ C) white or red wine*

Using a pointed knife, insert the halved or quartered garlic along the bone. Place meat in an ovenproof casserole. Heat the butter in a separate pan and pour over the meat. Bake on all sides in a 200° C (390° F) oven. Sprinkle with salt and pepper. Add the onion and after 10 minutes, half of the wine. Baste frequently with the liquid. Gradually pour in the rest of the wine. After 40 minutes turn off the heat, but leave the meat in the oven for another 5 minutes. The meat should be pink, not well done.
Note: Use a meat thermometer to be sure of accurate results.

## Fribourg Lamb Ragout

*1 kg (2.2 lbs) shoulder of lamb, 2 onions, 1 sprig*
*thyme, 3 garlic cloves, 1 bay leaf, 2½ dl (1 C) red*
*wine, 2 Tbs butter, 100 g (3½ oz) grapes, 2 cloves,*
*1 sage leaf, salt, pepper, 1 dl (⅓ C) cream (as desired),*
*1 Tbs flour (as desired)*

Cut the meat into 1½ inch cubes and place in a deep bowl. Chop the onion and add along with the thyme, 2 split garlic cloves and ½ bay leaf to the meat. Pour in enough red wine to cover the meat. Cover and let stand in refrigerator for 3 days. Turn occasionally.
Drain the meat and pat dry with paper towelling. Sauté on all sides in hot butter. Rub the marinade through a sieve and pour into a small bowl. Add the grapes. Stick the remaining onion with the ½ bay leaf and clove and add, together with the sage, to the meat. Then add the marinade/grape mixture and the pressed remaining garlic clove. Season with salt and pepper. Cover and simmer for 50-60 minutes. The meat should be tender, but not so tender that it falls apart.

Remove the meat from the saucepan and keep warm. Reduce the stock at high heat for 3-4 minutes. As desired, add the mixed flour and cream. Simmer and stir until the sauce is creamy but not too thick. This is served with small, round caramelized pears, known as "Poires à botzi".

## Emmental Shoulder of Lamb

This is a delicious lamb ragout, discreetly seasoned with saffron, traditionally served during "Sichlete", which is similar to Thanksgiving. In this area, saffron is also added to the meat stock, giving it a rather unique flavor.

*600 g (21 oz) deboned shoulder of lamb, 1/2 calf's foot, 2 Tbs butter, 1 onion, 1 rib celery, 1 carrot, 1/2 leek, 4 dl (1 1/2 C) bouillon, salt, pepper, nutmeg, 1 bay leaf, 1 clove, 1 Tbs flour, 1 dl (1/3 C) wine, 1 pinch saffran, 1 egg yolk, 1 dl (1/3 C) cream or milk*

Cut the meat into chunks and sauté together with the calf's foot on all sides in butter. Chop the onion, celery and carrot and slice the leek diagonally. Add to the meat and steam briefly. Pour in the bouillon and season with salt, pepper and nutmeg. Add the bay leaf and clove. Simmer for 45 minutes over low heat. Mix the flour and saffran with the wine and add to the meat. Let thicken. Beat the egg yolk with the cream or milk and pour into the pan as well. Scald. Remove saucepan from heat and season to taste. Serve with mashed potatoes.

47

# Fondue Bourguignonne
## (Meat Fondue)

This dish has nothing to do with the traditional Swiss fondue. It probably got its name from the fact that the meat pieces are cooked in a pot the same way as the bread is dipped into the cheese for cheese fondue.

> *Per person: 180 g (6 oz) tender beef (fillet or sirloin), cut into 2 x 2 cm (1 inch) dice, 3-4 dl (1¹/₄-1¹/₂ C) oil, eg. peanut oil, variety of cold sauces, mixed pickles, pearl onions etc., fresh rolls or potato chips, tossed salad*

Heat the oil in a special deep metal pot. Place in the center of the table over an alcohol lamp or electric warmer. Impale the cubes one at a time on special forks or wooden skewers and hold it in the hot oil. Leave it in for a longer or shorter period of time depending on whether the meat is preferred rare or well done. Place the meat on your plate and eat it with a separate fork. The fork used to cook the meat is much too hot!

Note: Although this specialty neither originates in Switzerland nor in Burgundy, it is a definite favorite. It's a great way to spend an evening with friends.

# Fricassée à la Vaudoise

In Vaud, this dish is prepared on the day of a slaughter. As opposed to the Geneva version, it does not use blood.

> *180 g (6 oz) pork, 1 small pig's foot, 1 Tbs pork fat, 1 carrot, 1 piece celery root, 1 tomato, 1 leek, 1 onion, 1 bunch parsley, 1 bay leaf, 1 clove, salt, pepper, 2 dl (³/₄ C) white wine, 1 Tbs grape schnaps*

Cut the meat into pieces. Sear the pieces and the pig's foot in pork fat. Slice celery, carrot, leek and tomato. Chop the onion. Add all vegetables to the meat and simmer. Add the unchopped parsley, bay leaf and clove. Season the meat with salt and pepper. Pour in wine and continue to simmer covered for 1½ hours. Add more water or wine if needed. Just before serving, sprinkle with schnaps.

Note: If a large amount of sauce is desired, add proportionately more liquid and bind shortly before serving with kneaded butter.

# Zurich Geschnetzeltes

This is the most popular Swiss dish. No visitor leaves (or should leave) Switzerland without having been served Geschnetzeltes. Variations either include veal kidneys or mushrooms (champignons).

*600 g (21 oz) veal, if possible sliced by hand, 2 Tbs butter, salt, pepper, 1 onion, 2 dl (¾ C) white wine, 2 dl (¾ C) cream, a few drops of lemon juice, 1 Tbs chopped parsley*

Sauté the thinly sliced veal on all sides in very hot butter. Remove from the pan, sprinkle with salt and pepper and keep warm. Slightly reduce the heat, then finely chop the onions and add them to the fat from the meat. Sauté briefly then pour in the wine. Simmer until the liquid is reduced by ½. Add the cream and bring to a boil. Then add the meat juices and season with salt, pepper and a few drops of lemon juice. Reheat the meat in the sauce but do not let it boil. Serve topped with parsley.

Note: Geschnetzeltes is traditionally accompanied by rösti (see page 66), but it is delicious with pasta as well.

# Pot-au-Feu

This dish serves as the opening of the voluminous festive meal named "Bénichon" in Freiburg. It is followed by lamb, ham shank, sausages with cabbage and beans, leg of lamb with mashed potatoes and red beet salad and finally, cheese, followed by delicious Gruyère double cream with blackberries, meringues and cookies for dessert.

49

This giant meal is offered in various country inns in early October throughout the canton of Freiburg.

*800 g (1½ lbs) shank or chuck beef, salt, 1 onion,*
*1 bay leaf, 1 clove, 1 small turnip, 1 leek, 6 carrots,*
*1 celery root, 1 small head cabbage, 4 potatoes, 50 g*
*(2 oz) grated Gruyère cheese*

Bring 2½ L (2½ qts) water to a boil. Add salt, then the meat. Stick the onion with the bay leaf and clove and add to the water. After 10 minutes, skim off the foam. Simmer gently for 1½ hours. Clean the vegetables. Quarter the cabbage, slice the leek in half, leave the carrots and celery whole and cut the turnip into slices. Add to the meat. Simmer for 30 more minutes. Cut the potatoes Parisienne style (relatively thick slices) and add to the meat. Simmer 20 minutes longer.

Before serving, slice the meat and serve on a warm platter with the vegetables. Cover with aluminum foil and place on a warmer while the soup is eaten topped with grated cheese.

Serve the meat with mustard, pickles or cornichons, pearl onions and cranberry sauce as desired.

*Good for company*

## Kid Ragout

This is a typical preparation of goat, usually served at Easter in the mountain regions of Ticino.

*1 kg (2.2 lbs) kid, cut in pieces, 2 Tbs butter, 50 g*
*(2 oz) diced lean bacon, 1 onion, salt, pepper, 1 sprig*
*sage, 1 sprig rosemary, 1 dl (⅓ C) Marsala, bouillon*
*as desired*

Brown the meat pieces on all sides in hot butter. Add the bacon and chopped onion and sauté. Sprinkle with salt and pepper and add the herb sprigs. Pour in the Marsala and simmer for about 1 hour. Add bouillon from time to time if necessary. Remove the pieces when the meat is tender. Set aside and keep warm. Deglaze the pan juices with some water or bouillon and let thicken. Season to taste. Pour over the meat.

# Jambon "à l'Os"
## (Boiled Ham)

This is how ham is prepared in Vaud.

### 10 and more servings

*1 whole, cured ham shank, approx. 4 kg (9 lbs),*
*1 onion stuck with 1 clove and 1 bay leaf*

Place the ham in a large, deep dish, cover with cold water and soak for 24 hours. Place in a large saucepan with water and the onion and simmer for about 3½ hours. Remove the rind. Serve hot or cold with mustard.

# Ham in Bread Dough

This is how eastern Swiss "dress up" their ham. It is taken to the baker to be cooked in his large oven and picked up again when it's done.

### 10 servings

*1 whole ham (4-5 kg / 9-11 lbs), preferably boneless,*
*2 Tbs brown sugar, 2 Tbs white wine, 5 Tbs mustard,*
*3 kg (6½ lbs) dark bread dough*

Place the ham in a deep saucepan, cover with water and cook 1-1½ hours. Remove and carefully pull off the rind. Brush with a mixture of sugar, wine and mustard. Roll out the dough 1 cm (⅓ in) thick and wrap around the ham. Place the ham face down on the dough and fold up the edges, allowing them to overlap. Dampen the edges with water and carefully press together. Place the "package" on a baking sheet so that the seam is on the bottom. Let rest for 30 minutes, then bake in a 170° C (338° F) preheated oven for 4 hours. If the crust turns too dark, cover it with aluminum foil. Leave the ham in the oven for 10 minutes after turning off the heat. Note: If white bread dough is used, the surface must be brushed with egg before baking. The dark dough need only be brushed with water and basted from time to time. To serve, use a sharp knife and cut out a large enough hole so that the ham can be lifted out. Cut the ham into slices and return, in its original form to the dough. Serve each piece of meat with a slice of bread.

51

## Short Rib Roast

*800 g (1½ lbs) deboned short ribs of veal, salt, pepper, nutmeg, sage, rosemary, 2 Tbs butter, 1 onion, 1 bay leaf, 1 clove, 2 carrots, ¼ L (1 C) white wine*

Dust the meat on all sides with pepper, nutmeg, sage and rosemary. Heat the butter in an ovenproof casserole. Add the meat and sear on both sides. Place in a preheated 240° C (465° F) oven and bake for 20 minutes. Salt the meat and bake for 15 minutes more. Reduce heat to 180° C (365° F). Stick the onion with the bay leaf and clove, peel and halve the carrots. Add to the meat. Heat the wine in a small saucepan and from time to time trickle 1-2 Tbs over the meat. Turn the meat occasionally. Leave the oven door ajar for the steam to escape. It is important that the meat be juicy and tender, but with a crisp crust on the outside. After a total baking time of 1½ hours, remove the meat from the oven. Deglaze the stock with 2-3 Tbs water and bring to a boil. Season to taste and reduce slightly.
Serve the rib roast on a plank in 1 cm (⅓ in) thick slices. Serve the sauce separately. Accompany with mashed potatoes or potato salad.

## Creamed Veal Scallopini

Creamed scallopini are just about as popular in Switzerland as "Geschnetzeltes". Below is a traditional recipe, although I leave out the flour and cornstarch.

*600 g (21 oz) veal, salt, pepper, 2 Tbs butter, ½ dl (2 Tbs) white wine, 2 dl (¾ C) cream*

Season the scallopini with salt and pepper and sauté on both sides in hot butter. Place on a platter and keep warm. Deglaze the pan juice with the white wine, add the cream and simmer for a few minutes until the sauce becomes thick and creamy. Season to taste. Add the meat juices and then pour over the scallopini.
Note: You may use pork instead of veal, and if desired, serve 1 larger scallopini per person instead of 2-3 small ones. Or, reduce the amount of meat and add mushrooms and a piece of butter before deglazing the pan juices. Then continue with the above preparation of the sauce.

## Veal Scallopini with Cheese

*4 veal scallopini, salt, pepper, 1 Tbs butter, butter for
the baking dish, 2-4 slices ham (depending on size),
4 slices Swiss cheese, 1½ dl (½ C) white wine*

Sauté the scallopini in butter until golden brown. Grease an oven-proof platter with butter. Season the meat on both sides with salt and pepper and lay side by side (or slightly touching if necessary) on the platter. Place a whole or half slice of ham on the veal. Top with slice of cheese. Place in a preheated 200° C (390° F) oven and bake until the cheese melts. Deglaze the pan juices with the white wine. Bring to a boil and allow to thicken. Pour over the meat before serving. Depending on the sharpness of the cheese, sprinkle with additional salt and pepper to taste.

## Pork Roast

*800 g (1½ lbs) pork roast, salt, pepper, 4 Tbs mus-
tard, 4 Tbs butter, 2 dl white wine, 2 dl (¾ C) bouillon, 3 carrots, 1 onion, 1 kg (2.2 lbs) small, new potatoes, 2 Tbs butter*

Sprinkle the meat with salt and pepper and brush generously with mustard. Place in an ovenproof casserole. Heat butter until very hot and pour over the meat. Bake in a preheated 200° C (390° F) oven. After 10 minutes add the wine and continue to bake, basting frequently. If necessary, add bouillon from time to time. Chop the carrots and onion. After 1 hour arrange the vegetables around the roast. Leave in for 30 more minutes. Boil the unpeeled scrubbed potatoes

53

in a small amount until semi-tender. Drain. Sauté in the remaining butter until light brown. Add to the meat 5 minutes before serving and cover with gravy.

Note: If small, new potatoes are not available, use larger ones cut into 4 pieces. These, however, must be peeled.

## Appenzell Pigs' Knuckles

*4-8 pigs' knuckles (depending on size), 1 tsp flour, 2 Tbs butter, salt, pepper, 1 small celery root, 1 carrot, 1 leek, 1 onion, 2 dl (³/₄ C) red wine, sage, marjoram, 3 Tbs tomato paste, 4 dl (1¹/₂ C) bouillon*

Dust the knuckles with flour. Heat the butter and sauté in it the meat on all sides. Sprinkle with salt and pepper. Peel and dice the celery and carrot. Slice the leek and coarsely chop the onion. Add the vegetables to the meat. Steam for a few minutes, then douse with the wine. Add sage, marjoram and tomato paste. Cover the pot and simmer gently for 1¹/₂-2 hours. Baste occasionally.

## Marinated Pork

During the carnival period, in the area between Lucerne and Bern there is a lot of card playing. The losers have to buy the winners this dish.

*1¹/₂ kg (3 lbs) pork (shoulder), 2 Tbs butter, 1-3 Tbs flour, 3 dl (1¹/₄ C) red wine or bouillon, salt, nutmeg, pepper, marjoram, butter for baking dish, 1 kg (2.2 lbs) brown bread dough, 1 egg white, 2 dl (³/₄ C) pig's blood (as desired)*

*Marinade: 4 dl (1¹/₂ C) red wine, 2 dl (³/₄ C) vinegar, 1 onion, 1 bay leaf, 2 cloves, 1 carrot, 1 leek, 6 peppercorns*

Combine and cook all given ingredients for the marinade. Cut the meat into chunks. Place in a dish and pour over the marinade. Let stand 2-3 days, turning occasionally.

Drain the meat and pat dry with paper towelling. Sauté on all sides in butter. Drain the vegetables and add to the meat. After 2-3 minutes, dust with flour, turn and pour in 3 dl (1¹/₄ C) liquid (marinade, red wine or bouillon). Season with salt, pepper, nutmeg and marjoram. Cover and simmer over low heat for 30-40 minutes. Place the meat in a straight-sided oven proof baking dish. Roll out the dough and place it on top of the dish. Use egg white to stick it around the edges of the dish. Use a fork to make a small "escape hole" for the steam. Bake at 220° C (428° F) for 30-40 minutes until the crust is brown and crisp.

This dish may also be prepared without a cover of dough. In that case, use less flour. When the meat is done, stir the blood into the sauce. Do not boil, this would cause it to clot. The blood will make the sauce very dark. It is not advisable to use blood if you do choose to make a dough cover as the heat in the oven will cause the blood to clot as well.

## Geneva Marinated Pork

*800 g (1½ lbs) pork, 1 pig's foot cut into pieces*
*Marinade: 2 carrots, 1 piece cellery root, 2 onions,*
*2 garlic cloves, 1 large bay leaf, 1 sprig thyme, 1 clove,*
*2 sprigs parsley, 5 peppercorns, marjoram, 1 bottle*
*red wine, 2 Tbs butter or pork fat, 2 Tbs flour, 1½ dl*
*(½ C) cream, 1 dl (⅓ C) pork blood*

Cut the meat into chunks. Clean and dice the vegetables. Combine all ingredients for the marinade in a bowl, add the meat and pig's foot and pour in the wine. Cover and let stand in a cool place for 3 days. Turn once or twice daily, always making sure that the meat is completely covered with liquid.

Drain the meat and pig's foot and pat dry with paper towelling. Sauté on all sides in hot fat or butter. Dust with flour and simmer for 5 minutes. Meanwhile, bring the marinade to a boil and reduce just a bit. Rub through a sieve and add to the meat. Cover and place in a 170° C (338° F) oven for 1½ hours. Remove the meat and foot pieces and keep warm. Reduce stock further, add the cream and let thicken for 2-3 minutes. Remove from heat and stir in the blood. Do not let boil. Pour the sauce over the meat and serve.

Note: The blood could be left out, but it is a customary ingredient in Geneva.

55

## Stufato al Merlot
## (Beef Pot Roast)

*1 kg (2.2 lbs) chuck, salt, pepper, ¹/₂ pig's foot, 2 Tbs butter, 1 carrot, 1 piece celery root, 1 small leek, 1 onion, 1 bay leaf, 1 clove, ¹/₄ L (1 C) red wine (Merlot), 2 garlic cloves, 1 bouquet herbs consisting of 1 sprig each rosemary, sage, marjoram, 1-2 dl (¹/₃-³/₄ C) bouillon, 2 dl (³/₄ C) instant gravy*

Rub meat with pepper and sear with pig's foot on all sides in the fat. Dice the carrots and celery and slice the leek. Stick the onion with the bay leaf and clove. Add all vegetables to meat and simmer. Add red wine, pressed garlic and herbs. Allow liquid to thicken, then cover and simmer gently for 2 hours. The meat should be very tender. Remove meat and wrap in aluminum foil to keep warm. Add instant gravy to the pot liquor and bring to a boil. Season to taste with salt and pepper.

Cut into slices and serve garnished with the vegetables. Serve with polenta (see page 104) or risotto (see page 105).

Note: If a juicier roast is prefered, use a larded piece of meat. (Have the butcher do it for you!)

## Suubäggli
## (Ham Shank)

In many places cooked or fried ham is the main part of a holiday meal. The canton of Schwyz has especially original ways of preparing this favorite piece of meat.

6-8 servings — depending on size of shank

*1 boneless shank (pre-cooked), 10 small bay leaves, 10 cloves*

Remove the rind from the ham while still warm. If you buy it already cooked, the butcher will take care of this for you.

Score the outer fatty layer into a diamond pattern with a pointed knife and stick in the bay leaves and cloves. Place in a baking dish and bake in a 200° C (390° F) preheated oven for 30-35 minutes. Carve at the table.

Note: This ham is traditionally accompanied by "Suuri Gummeli" (see page 71). Count on 200-250 g (7-9 oz) ham per person.

# Mixed Fillets and Vegetables

In the old guildhalls of Zurich, this is served by the name of "Zürcher Ratsherrentopf".

> *400 g (14 oz) fresh peas (or ½ can), 300 g (10½ oz) carrots, 3 Tbs butter, 400 g (14 oz) potatoes, salt, pepper, majoram, thyme, 4 slices veal-, beef-, pork fillet, veal kidney, calf liver, lean bacon, 4 small link sausages*

Hull the peas. Peel and slice the carrot. Sauté both in 1 Tbs butter with 1-2 Tbs water added until tender (canned vegetables need only be drained and heated). Peel and finely dice potatoes. Sauté in 1 Tbs butter until golden brown and tender. Season peas and carrots with salt. Melt the remaining butter in a large saucepan. In it sauté the meat and sausages briefly on both sides (start with the sausages, they take the longest to be done). Season with salt, pepper, marjoram and thyme. Arrange peas, carrots and potatoes on a large platter and place the meat on top. Serve at once.

Note: This dish looks especially appetizing if the meat is prepared on a grill instead of in a frying pan. If you do choose to grill the meat, brush it beforehand with some melted butter.

## b) Innards

In the past, the people of Switzerland ate innards out of frugality. Nothing was ever wasted after a slaughter, and consequently the Swiss cuisine has many recipes including tripe, kidneys, liver and chitlings; recipes which today are especially cherished by gourmets. In addition to many hearty innards specialities, which are usually made with pork, there are also more refined preparations such as the Zurich liver kebabs with sage or the "Geschnetzeltes" mixed with thinly sliced kidneys. If the sauce is made properly, these dishes can easily compete amongst the best.

## Liver Kebabs

*500 g (1 lb) calf liver, 100 g (3½ oz) lean bacon (4 slices), 8-12 sage leaves, 2 Tbs butter, salt, pepper, 3 Tbs bouillon*

Slice the liver 1½ cm (½ in) thick. Cut these slices into 3 x 3 cm (1 in) pieces. Divide each slice of bacon into 3 pieces. Alternate the liver cubes, bacon and sage on skewers. Grill the kebabs on all sides in a frying pan with hot butter until brown and crisp. Remove from pan, season with salt and pepper. Cover and set aside to keep warm. Add the bouillon to the drippings, let thicken and pour over the kebabs. Note: In the original recipe, the kebabs are served on a bed of green beans and bacon. The sauce is poured over as a final touch.

## Sautéed Calf Liver

*500 g (1 lb) calf liver, 2 Tbs butter, 1 onion, 1 Tbs chopped parsley, salt, pepper, 50 g (4 Tbs) fresh butter, 1 pinch each marjoram and thyme*

Cut the liver into thin slices. Heat 1 Tbs butter and sauté the finely chopped onion until translucent (about 10 minutes). Add the parsley and sauté 1-2 minutes. In another pan, gently heat the remaining butter and add the liver. Sauté until it loses its red color, turning constantly. Season with salt and pepper and add the onions. Place on a

hot platter and keep warm. Quickly melt the fresh butter. Add marjoram and thyme, then trickle over the liver. Serve at once.
Note: The Swiss serve this dish with rösti (see page 66).

## Zurich Style Tripe

*600 g (1 lb 5 oz) cooked tripe, 2 onions, 1 leek, 1 carrot, 2 Tbs butter, 1 Tbs flour, 2 dl (³/₄ C) white wine, 2 dl (³/₄ C) bouillon, salt, pepper, ¹/₂ tsp caraway, 1 bay leaf*

Cut the tripe into squares or strips. Cut the onions and leek into rings. Peel the carrot. Sauté in butter onions, leek and carrot. Dust with flour and pour in the white wine. Add the tripe followed by the bouillon. Season with salt, pepper and caraway and add the bay leaf. Cover and simmer gently for 1 hour. Before serving remove the carrot and the bay leaf.
Note: In Switzerland this dish is served with peeled or unpeeled boiled potatoes.

## Neuchâtel Tripe  *Different, but good!*

*800 g (1¹/₂ lbs) cooked tripe, ¹/₂ L (2 C) white wine, 2¹/₂ dl (1 C) bouillon, 1 onion, 1 bay leaf, 1 clove, 1 carrot, 1 leek, 1 piece celery root, 5 peppercorns, salt, majoram, thyme*
*For the Sauce Vinaigrette: 2 Tbs wine vinegar, 1 Tbs sharp mustard, 8 Tbs oil, salt, ground pepper, 2 Tbs chopped herbs (parsley, chives, rosemary, thyme, marjoram), 2 cornichons or regular pickles, 1 tsp capers, 1 small onion*

Cut the tripe into large squares, approx. 5 x 5 cm (2 x 2 in). Bring the wine and bouillon to a boil. Stick the onion with the bay leaf and clove and add to the wine along with the cleaned, coarsely chopped vegetables. Add some salt. Add the tripe and cover. Simmer for about 1 hour on low heat. Mix the mustard, vinegar and oil for the Sauce Vinaigrette. Add the finely chopped pickles, capers and onion. Add the herbs and stir well. Season with a generous amount of salt and pepper.
When the tripe is very tender, place the pot on the table.
Serve with the Sauce Vinaigrette and boiled potatoes in their jackets.

## c) Poultry and Game

Every farmer's wife still has her own chicken coop. This is her realm, and custom has it that whatever money she earns off her chickens is hers. Traditionally only served on Sundays, the preparation of tasty chicken ("Guggeli") dishes goes a long way back. Until well into the fifties, chicken was considered a festive dish. Today it is prepared in a variety of different ways, and pricewise, it has become a welcome everyday meal.

Every year in the fall, it is hunting season in our forests and mountains, and everyone looks forward to delicious venison specialities. The hunter bring the mountain goats down into the valleys where the meat is then prepared according to the old recipes of the mountain cantons.

## Chicken à la Grandma

### 2 servings

*1 fresh chicken (approx. 900 g/2 lbs), 3 Tbs butter,
1 small piece of celery, 1 carrot, ½ leek, 1 onion, 1 dl
(⅓ C) white wine, 1 bay leaf, 3 dl (1¼ C) bouillon,
salt, pepper, 1 Tbs mustard*

Draw the chicken. Cut off neck and feet. Clean the stomach, liver and heart. Place the feet in boiling water. Allow to boil for 5 minutes. Let cool and pull off the skin. Sauté the skinned feet with the neck, stomach, liver and heart in 1 Tbs butter. Dice the celery, carrot, leek and onion. Add to the meat. Pour in white wine. Add the bay leaf and bouillon. Simmer for 2 hours. Rub the chicken inside and out generously with salt and pepper. Using the remaining butter, bake in a 250° C (482° F) oven on all sides. Brush with mustard. Reduce heat to 180° C (356° F) and roast for another 30 minutes. Pass the prepared viscera, neck and feet through a strainer. Add to the chicken drippings and let thicken slightly. Season with salt and pepper. Serve the sauce separately.

# Mistkratzerli
## (Baby Chicken)

*2 broilers 600-800 g (1-1½ lbs) each or 1 fryer, 100 g
(3½ oz) each finely ground veal and pork, 50 g (2 oz)
finely chopped bacon, salt, pepper, marjoram, 50 g
(2 oz) lean bacon in thin slices, 1½ dl (½ C) white
wine, 2 dl (¾ C) bouillon, 1 tsp flour, 80 g (2¾ oz)
butter, 100 g (3½ oz) pearl onions, 100 g (3½ oz)
small mushrooms (champignons)*

Mix the ground meat with the salt, pepper, marjoram and half of the wine. Rub the chicken inside and out with salt and pepper. Stuff with the meat mixture and secure. Bard with the bacon. Cook in half of the butter until golden brown. Add the rest of the wine, then bake in a 180° C (356° F) oven for 35 minutes, basting frequently. Sauté the onions and mushrooms in butter with the bouillon and add to the chicken. Bake another 15 minutes.

Knead the flour with 1 tsp butter. Remove the chicken and bind the drippings with the kneaded butter. Cut the chicken in half and slice the stuffing. Dress the chicken halves with the stuffing, mushrooms and onions. Taste the sauce, season if necessary, and pour over the chicken.


# Coniglio Arrosto
## (Braised Rabbit)

*1 kg (2.2 lbs) rabbit, cut into pieces, 2 Tbs butter,
100 g (3½ oz) lean, diced bacon, 1 carrot, 1 onion,
2 garlic cloves, salt, pepper, 1 bay leaf, 2 cloves, 3 dl
(1¼ C) red wine, 1-2 dl (⅓-¾ C) bouillon, 3-4 sage
leaves*

Sauté the pieces of meat on all sides together with the bacon. Add the sliced carrot, onion and pressed garlic. Season with salt and pepper, add bay leaf and pour in wine. Cover and simmer at low heat for 1 hour. Turn the meat from time to time. Add bouillon as needed. Note: If you want a lot of sauce, add more bouillon and bind with a bit of tomato paste or instant gravy. The sauce is especially tasty if you add a few dried (pre-soaked in water) mushrooms.

# Marinated Venison

## 6-8 servings

*2 kg (4 lbs) venison (with bones), 2 Tbs butter, 1 carrot, 1 piece celery root, 1 Tbs flour, salt, pepper, 2 dl (³/₄ C) venison or pork blood (as desired), 4 Tbs cream*
*Marinade: 5 dl (2 C) red wine, ¹/₂ dl (2 Tbs) red wine vinegar, 1 onion, 1 bay leaf, 1 clove, a few juniper berries, 4 garlic cloves, 2 carrots, 2-3 sage leaves*

Cut the meat into chunks. Combine and cook all given ingredients for marinade. (Chop the onions and carrots and press the garlic.) Pour the hot or cold marinade over the meat. Let stand 8-10 days. Turn daily and make sure that the meat is always completely covered with liquid.

Drain the meat and pat dry with paper towelling. Sauté on all sides in hot butter. Add the peeled and diced carrot and the celery root. Briefly steam the vegetables, then dust with flour. Pour in a portion of the strained marinade. Season with salt and pepper. Cover and simmer for 1-1½ hours until tender.

Remove the meat and keep warm. Bring the sauce to a boil. Simmer until reduced by about ³/₄, add the cream and boil again. Remove from the heat and stir in blood as desired. Do not let boil again. Pour over the meat.

Note: For an especially elegant preparation of this dish, add sautéed chanterelles and fried bacon bits shortly before serving.

# Venison Cutlets with Mushrooms

*200 g (7 oz) chanterelles, 1 onion, 500 g (1 lb) venison cutlets, 2 Tbs flour, 2 Tbs butter, salt, pepper, 4 Tbs white wine, 1 Tbs chopped parsley, 1¹/₂ dl (¹/₂ C) cream*

Clean the mushrooms and cut into halves or quarters depending on their size. Finely chop the onion. Dust the meat lightly with flour and sauté on both sides in 1 Tbs butter. Season with salt and pepper. Remove from pan and keep warm. Melt the remaining butter and add the mushrooms and onions. Sauté. Pour in the white wine. Season with salt and pepper and add the parsley. Add the cream and cook for a few minutes. Pour the sauce over the venison and serve at once.

# Notes and more recipes

fig. 5

# Potato Dishes

During the hard times, the potato was the main source of food in Switzerland as well as in the surrounding countries. It is no wonder that so many different potato dishes were created, mainly by inventive housewives. The simplest recipe is for "Gschwellti". These are potatoes boiled in their jackets and served with butter and cheese. Another typical example is "Rösti" which, depending on the region, are prepared with bacon or onions. In the past, they were fried in lard, but today one prefers butter. Rösti are a perfect accompaniment for Zurich Geschnetzeltes or calf's liver.

# Rösti
## (Swiss Fried Potatoes)

In itself rösti is a very simple dish, but the preparation takes some know how. It is important that the potatoes be cooked at least one day beforehand. They must be pressed together in the pan like a round loaf and covered with a soup bowl or a tightly fitting lid. Rösti must not be stirred, otherwise they will not form a crust.

*1 kg (2.2 lbs) potatoes, 3 Tbs butter, 1 tsp salt, 2 Tbs milk*

Boil the unpeeled potatoes until semi-tender the day before preparation. Peel and grate, using a grater with fairly large holes. Heat the butter in a skillet. Add the potatoes and sprinkle with salt. Using a spatula, press into a round loaf. Sprinkle with milk and cover securely. Reduce the heat as soon as the potatoes begin to sizzle. Fry very slowly for another 30 minutes. During this time a brown crust will form. Cover the pan with a flat platter and flip the rösti onto it.

**Rösti Variations**
Rösti can also be prepared from raw, finely grated potatoes. Turn a few times in hot butter, then press into a loaf and cover. Fry for 15-20 minutes.
Rösti with Bacon: Finely chop lean bacon and sauté in butter. Add to potatoes.
Rösti with Onions: Cut onions into strips. Fry with the potatoes.

Rösti with Cheese: This recipe is often used in the mountain cantons of Switzerland. Add thinly sliced rich cheese to the potatoes. Enhance with onions and/or bacon as desired.

## Rösti à la Jurassienne

*1 kg (2.2 lbs) potatoes, boiled the previous day, 3 Tbs
butter, 1 onion, salt, pepper, 150 g (5 oz) lean bacon,
250 g (9 oz) Gruyère (or any hard cheese)*

Peel and grate the potatoes. In a skillet, heat 2 Tbs butter and in it sauté the coarsley chopped onion. Add the potatoes. Season with salt and pepper. Grease an ovenproof baking dish and fill evenly with the potatoes. Cover with the bacon and sliced cheese. Place in a preheated 180° C (356° F) oven. Bake until the cheese has melted and the bacon is crisp.

## Potato Gratin

*1 kg (2.2 lbs) potatoes, 2 large onions, salt, pepper,
butter for baking dish, 100 g (3¹/₂ oz) grated Gruyère
cheese, 2 dl (³/₄ C) white wine, 2 dl (³/₄ C) cream*

Cut potatoes into thin slices and chop the onions. Place in a bowl and sprinkle with salt and pepper. Mix well. Grease an ovenproof baking dish. Add in layers, the potato mixture and the grated cheese. Mix the wine with 1 dl (¹/₃ C) water and pour in dish. Cover with aluminum foil and bake for 75 minutes in a 180° C (356° F) preheated oven. When the potatoes are tender, pour in the cream. Bake, uncovered, for an additional 15 minutes.

# Kartoffelpfluten
## (Potato Dumplings)

*1 kg (2.2 lbs) potatoes, 4 dl (1½ C) milk, salt, nutmeg,*
*2 eggs, 3 Tbs flour, 6 Tbs bread crumbs, 70-100 g*
*(2½-3½ oz) butter*

Peel the boiled potatoes while still warm. Put through a ricer. Add the heated milk, salt and nutmeg. Mix well with a whisk. Let cool. Beat the eggs and add, along with the flour to the potatoes. Stir into a semi-firm dough. Add flour or milk as needed. Using a wet spoon, slowly drop balls of dough into simmering salted water. Remove the dumplings with a colander as soon as they rise to the surface. Drain well and place on a hot platter. Set aside and keep warm. When all the dough is used up, lightly brown the bread crumbs in butter and sprinkle over the dumplings. Serve with apple or pear slices and white coffee.
Note: Mix grated cheese into the potato mixture as desired.

## Potatoes with Cheese

*6 large, unpeeled potatoes, butter for baking dish,*
*1 onion, 1 tsp butter, 1½ dl (½ C) white wine, salt,*
*pepper, 1 garlic clove, 200 g (7 oz) raclette cheese*
*(semi-hard cheese), freshly ground pepper*

Peel and dice the potatoes. Chop the onions and sauté in butter. Add potatoes. After a few minutes, add the vine. Cover and simmer over low heat for 15 minutes. Grease an ovenproof baking dish with butter. Fill the dish with the potatoes. Top with pressed garlic. Cut the cheese into very thin slices and arrange over potatoes. Place in a pre-heated 180° C (356° F) oven until the cheese has melted, but not changed color. Sprinkle with pepper.

# Gschwellti
## (Potatoes boiled in their jackets)

*1 kg (2.2 lbs) potatoes of equal size if possible, 1 tsp*
*salt*

Place the washed, unpeeled potatoes in a deep saucepan, cover with water and bring to a boil. Add salt and reduce the heat. Cover and cook for 20-25 minutes (depending on size and quality) until tender. Test for doneness with a pointed knife.

Note: Gschwellti are the basis for a popular Swiss dish known as Rösti. The potatoes should be boiled on the previous day. Served hot with cheese and butter, Gschwellti also make a quick and tasty dinner for the family.

## Maluns

*1 kg (2.2 lbs) unpeeled, day-old boiled potatoes, 400 g (3⅓ C) flour, salt, 150 g (5 oz) butter, 2 Tbs butter flakes*

Peel and grate the potatoes. Using your fingers mix potatoes and flour until the flour is absorbed. In a skillet, heat about 50 g (4 Tbs) butter and add the potato/flour mixture. Sprinkle with salt. Fry for 40 minutes, turning constantly. From time to time, add more butter. The mixture should form into small, crispy potato bits. Place on a warm platter and dot with butter.

Note: This dish needs a lot of attention, but it's worth it! Served with apple sauce and "mountain" cheese, it is a delicious meal.

# Ofetori

*4 portions firm, mashed potatoes, 30 g (2 Tbs) butter,*
*1 egg, 3 Tbs grated cheese, 200 g (7 oz) lean bacon,*
*butter for the baking dish, butter flakes*

Beat the egg and combine with mashed potatoes, melted butter and grated cheese. Pour into a well greased, straight sided ovenproof baking dish. Smooth out the surface with a knife or spatula. Cut the bacon first into 1 cm (⅓ in) thick slices, then into 1 cm (⅓ in) wide sticks. Spread over the mashed potatoes. Bake 15 minutes in a 180° C (356° F) preheated oven. Remove and dot with butter. Return to oven and bake for another 10-15 minutes.
Serve with plenty of salad.
Note: There are many varieties of this dish. In the canton of Zug for example it is customary to make a well in the mashed potatoes and fill it with grated cheese and bacon bits. Another recipe calls for the bacon to be stirred into the potatoes. Then, using a wet spoon, several wells are formed and each is filled with a raw egg.

# Pizokel

*6 potatoes, 250 g (9 oz) flour, 3 eggs, 2 dl (¾ C)*
*milk, salt, pepper, 50 g (4 Tbs) butter, 120 g (4 oz)*
*grated Parmesan or Sbrinz cheese*

Peel the raw potatoes and grate them into a bowl. Combine flour, beaten eggs, milk, 1 dl (⅓ C) water, salt and pepper and add to potatoes. Mix into a firm dough. If needed, add more flour. In a large saucepan, bring lightly salted water to a boil. Put the batter through a colander or spätzle cutter, or spread it on a wooden board and using a large knife, slide even strips of batter into the water. Simmer until the "Pizokels" rise to the surface. Remove from water and drain. Layer into a deep dish with the cheese. Lightly brown the butter and pour over the prepared Pizokels.
Note: You may wish to brown bread crumbs or onions in the butter before pouring it over the Pizokels. In the southern part of the canton of Graubünden Pizokels are enhanced with a variety of diced vegetables (carrots, beans, cabbage, celery etc.). The vegetables are

cooked in salted water until tender and arranged in a dish in alternate layers with the Pizokels and cheese. Everything is then topped with browned butter. With the vegetables this dish is transformed into a stew. Without vegetables, Pizokels are served with a meat dish.

*Hearty*

## Schnitz and Härdöpfel

*4 Tbs sugar, 750 g (1½ lbs) pears, 1 kg (2.2 lbs) potatoes, salt, 2 dl (¾ C) cream, 2 Tbs flour*

Brown the sugar in a saucepan. Add 5 dl (2 C) water. Peel and slice the pears. Place into the saucepan and cook until soft. In a separate pot, bring salted water to a boil and add the peeled, diced potatoes. Cook until the potatoes are tender. Drain and add to the pears. In a small dish, mix the cream with the flour and add to the pear/potato mixture. Bring to a boil and season to taste with salt or sugar.
Serve with hot sausages. Sometimes this dish is served with "green" (unsmoked) cooked bacon.

## Suuri Gummeli
## (Sour Potatoes)

*1 large onion, 1 Tbs butter, 1 kg (2.2 lbs) potatoes, 5 dl (2 C) bouillon, salt, pepper, nutmeg, 1 bay leaf, 2-3 tsp cream, 1½ Tbs flour, 1 Tbs vinegar, 1 Tbs chopped herbs (parsley, chives, marjoram)*

Chop the onions and sauté in butter. Peel the potatoes and cut into 2-3 cm (¾-1 in) thick slices. Add to the onions. Let draw for a few minutes, then pour in the bouillon. Season with salt, pepper and a tad of nutmeg. Add the bay leaf. Simmer for 12-15 minutes. Mix the cream with the flour. Add to potatoes when they are almost tender. Stir well and pour in vinegar. Let thicken for another 2-3 minutes. Season to taste. Careful: the potatoes must not fall apart. Top with the chopped herbs and serve.

71

# Gnocchi
## 6 servings

*1 kg (2.2 lbs) potatoes, 500 g (1 lb) flour, salt, pepper, nutmeg, 100 g (3½ oz) grated Parmesan or Sbrinz cheese*

Peel potatoes. Cut into pieces and boil in salted water until tender. Put through a ricer while still warm. Gradually work in the flour until you have a smooth dough. Dust a wooden board with flour and roll out the dough into sticks ½ inch thick. Cut into 3 cm (1 in) lengths. Drop batches of gnocchi into a large saucepan of simmering salted water. Let draw until they rise to the surface. Remove with a colander. Drain well. Arrange in layers with the cheese in a hot, deep platter. Cover with aluminum foil and keep warm until the next portion is ready.

Note: Gnocchi taste best if a tomato sauce is poured over them shortly before serving. The sauce may be prepared with tomato paste, fresh or canned tomatoes.

# Touetché
# (Flat Potato Cakes)

*1 kg (2.2 lbs) potatoes (preferably mealy), 100-150 g (1-1¼ C) flour, salt, pepper, nutmeg, 1½ dl (½ C) cream*

Boil the unpeeled potatoes until tender. Peel while still warm. Pass through a ricer. Season with salt, pepper and nutmeg. Mix with as much flour as necessary to get a fairly firm dough (similar to bread dough). Grease a baking sheet with butter and dust with flour. Roll out the dough on the sheet to 1-1½ cm (⅓-½ in) thickness. Using the back side of a knife or a brush, spread the cream over the surface of the dough. Bake in a preheated 180° C (356° F) oven, until the surface turns golden yellow (about 10-15 minutes). Cut into pieces before serving.

# Notes and more recipes

*fig. 6*

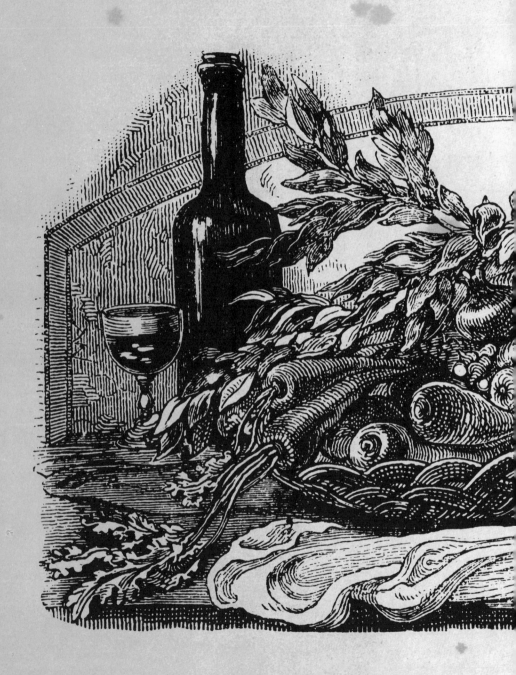

# Vegetables

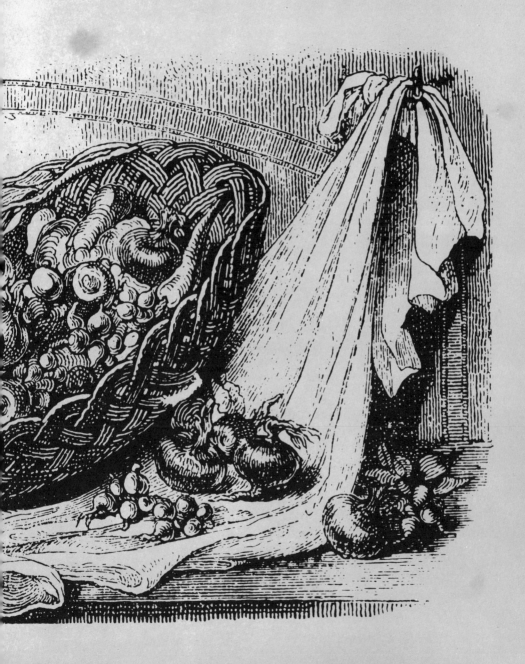

In Switzerland, vegetables appear either cooked or steamed as an accompaniment to a meat dish. There are, however, a number of original vegetable recipes, which can serve as the main part of a meal. A few of these recipes are described in the following chapter.

## Carrots with Bacon

This dish is served in Vaud during the wine harvest.

*600 g (21 oz) lean, smoked bacon, 1 kg (2.2 lbs) carrots, 1 onion, 2 Tbs butter, salt, pepper*

Cook the bacon in a small amount of water until halfway tender. Cut the carrots into small strips and chop the onion. Sauté both in butter. Add 1 Tbs water and season to taste with salt and pepper. Cover with the precooked bacon. Cover and simmer for 50-60 minutes. Before serving, cut the bacon into pieces and arrange over the carrots.

*Serve with a glass of Fendant*

## Mushroom Ragout

*1 kg (2.2 lbs) mushrooms (chanterelles, champignons, steinpilz), 1 large onion, 2 Tbs butter, salt, pepper, parsley, cream as desired, 50 g (4 Tbs) butter, 2 Tbs chopped parsley*

Clean the mushrooms. Depending on their shape, cut into halves, quarters or slices. Finely chop the onions and sauté in butter. Add the mushrooms and sauté until they are limp. Pour the juices into a small pan. Heat and reduce by half. Using a whisk, vigorously bind the sauce with flakes of butter. Season the mushrooms with salt and pepper and pour over the sauce.
Note: Only use fresh mushrooms, packed or controlled by reputable firms. A variety of mushrooms cooked together is especially good. This mushroom ragout is excellent with polenta (see page 104).

# Morels on Toast

In the fall, the Swiss forests boast an abundance of mushrooms. The morels, found in May on the slopes of the Jura or Rigi mountains, are a special favorite.

*40 (3 Tbs) dried or 400 g (14 oz) fresh morels, 2 Tbs finely chopped shallots, 2 Tbs butter, ½ Tbs flour, 3 Tbs white wine, salt, pepper, 2½ dl (1 C) cream, 4 slices white bread (French or Italian)*

Soak dried morels for 1 hour in warm water. Change the water frequently. Clean fresh morels thoroughly to remove all traces of sand. Depending on the size of the mushrooms, cut into halves or quarters. Sauté the shallots in 1 Tbs butter. Add the well drained mushrooms. Cover and steam for 10-15 minutes (dried morels a bit longer). Dust with flour and pour in the wine. Add the cream and allow to thicken over low heat. Season with salt and pepper. Sauté the bread in a skillet with the remaining butter on both sides until golden brown. Place each slice of toast on a separate plate and cover with mushrooms and sauce.

Note: In order to preserve the unique flavour of the morels, do not use lemon juice or substitute any other herbs for this dish.

# Mushroom Toast

*4 slices white bread (French or Italian), 2 Tbs butter, 4 slices cooked or raw ham, 4 thin slices Emmentaler cheese, 200 g (7 oz) chanterelles or other mushroom varieties, 1 Tbs flour, 4 Tbs white wine, 4 Tbs bouillon, salt, pepper, marjoram*

First toast the bread in a toaster, oven or frying pan. Place in a greased ovenproof baking dish. Dress with ham, then cheese and place in a 200° C (390° F) oven. Bake until the cheese melts. Meanwhile, clean the mushrooms. Cut into halves or quarters and sauté in butter. Dust with flour and add wine and bouillon. Season with salt, pepper and marjoram and cook for 10 minutes. Spread over the cheese sandwiches and serve immediately.

## Räbebappe
## (Turnip Stew)

The canton of Aargau has an abundance of turnips along with potatoes. Turnips thus are among the most important food staples of this canton. The recipe below is still frequently served, although no longer as a main meal.

*6-8 white turnips, salt, 2 Tbs butter, 1½ dl (½ C) cream, 1 pinch caraway*

Peel the turnips and cut into pieces. Simmer in salted water until tender. Drain the liquid. Allow the turnips to release some steam and remove from heat. Mash the turnips with a potato masher. Stir in butter, cream and caraway. Mix well and reheat.
Serve with Rösti or apple rings.


## Baked Asparagus

Asparagus thrive especially well in the Valais region. In the spring they are thus available in surplus amounts and are therefore not only cooked but prepared in a variety of other ways a well.

*1 kg (2.2 lbs) white asparagus, salt, pepper, 1 tsp sugar, 2½ Tbs butter, 2 Tbs flour, 2 dl (¾ C) cream, ½ dl (3 Tbs) bouillon as needed, 500 g (18 oz) tomatoes, butter for the pan, 50 g (2 oz) grated cheese*

Peel the asparagus generously. Cook in boiling, salted water together with the sugar and ½ tsp butter for 15-20 minutes depending upon quality of the asparagus. Melt the remaining butter and sauté in it the flour. Do not let it brown. Pour in 2 dl (¾ C) asparagus stock and simmer gently for 10 minutes. Add the cream and season with salt and pepper. If the sauce is too thick, you may dilute it with some bouillon. Slit the tomatoes crosswise at the top, plunge in boiling water for a few seconds and peel. Halve, press out the seeds and dice. Grease an ovenproof baking dish and layer it with the tomatoes. Cover with the asparagus. Pour over the white sauce and sprinkle with grated cheese. Bake in a hot oven at 200° C (390° F) until brown spots begin to show on the surface.

78

## Red Cabbage with Apples

### 6-8 servings

*1 red cabbage, 1 large onion, 2 Tbs butter, 2 apples,*
*2 dl (³/₄ C) red wine, 2-3 dl (³/₄-1¹/₄ C) bouillon, salt,*
*pepper, ¹/₂ tsp dillweed, ¹/₂ tsp caraway, 1 dash sugar,*
*2 Tbs wine vinegar*

Cut the cabbage head in half, remove the hard core and cut the leaves into fine strips. Finely chop the onion and sauté in the butter. Gradually add the cabbage, turning constantly. Sauté the cabbage until it is limp. After approx. 15 minutes add the wine. Pour in bouillon until the cabbage is covered. Add the grated, unpeeled apple. Season with salt, pepper, dill, caraway and sugar. Cover the pan and simmer the cabbage for 1¹/₂-2 hours. After this time the liquid should be absorbed. In the last 10 minutes, stir in the vinegar.
Note: This is an ideal accompaniment for pork roast or venison dishes.

79

fig · 7

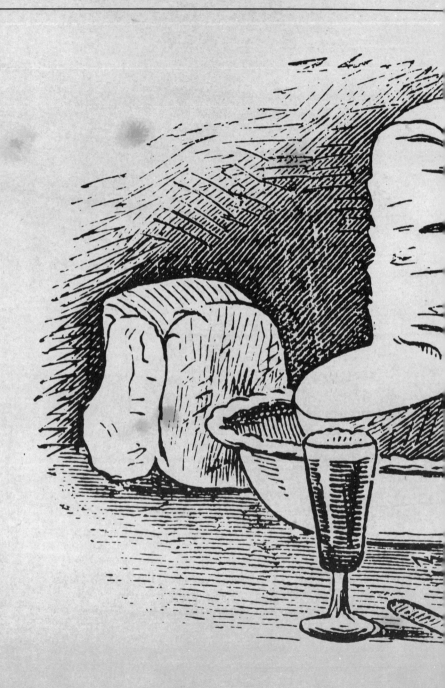

# Cheese and Egg Dishes

In the evening, the Swiss often prefer to eat a simple meal without meat, like any number of pancake variations or dishes made from stale bread, eggs and milk. Cheese dishes are also a popular light evening meal.

The Swiss cheese is world reknowned especially, of course, the Emmentaler and Gruyère. The cheese fondue has achieved worldwide popularity. But cheese is also used in other specialities such as cheese toasts, cheese soufflés and light cheesecakes.

## Alte Maa

("Old Man", a bread/cheese specialty from the canton of Appenzell)

*500 g (18 oz) day-old brown bread, 250 g (9 oz)*
*Appenzeller cheese, 2½ dl (1 C) milk, 3 Tbs butter*

Cut the bread into small pieces (slices or cubes) and layer in a deep dish alternately with the cheese. Mix the milk with the cream and pour over the bread. Let stand for 1 hour. The bread should absorb all the milk but not get mushy. Heat the butter in a frying pan, add the bread mixture and fry, turning occasionally, until crisp.

In Switzerland this dish is served with white coffee and/or a bowl of tossed salad.

Note: Add chopped onions to the bread mixture as desired.

## Amelette
## (Omelette, Swiss for pancake)

### Basic Recipe

*250 g (9 oz) flour, 2 dl (³/₄ C) milk, 2 dl (³/₄ C) water,*
*salt, 3-4 eggs, 3 Tbs butter*

Mix the flour, milk, water and salt in a bowl until smooth. Beat in the eggs with a whisk. The batter should be thick but smooth. Let stand for 30 minutes.

In a round skillet, melt a small lump of butter per pancake. Add a small ladleful of batter. Tip the skillet and let the batter spread over the bottom. When the pancake is golden brown underneath, reverse it and briefly cook the other side. Arrange on warm platter, either flat or folded depending on how you wish to serve them. Cover with aluminum foil and keep in a warm place.

Note: Using this basic recipe, you can prepare a wide variety of dishes. Fillings may be sweet or spicy such as apple sauce, fruit preserves, berries, sautéed mushrooms, vegetables, ground beef or meat leftovers.

## Egg Rösti

*300 g (10½ oz) stale brown bread, 2½ dl (1 C) milk,*
*3 Tbs butter, 4 eggs, salt*

Cut the bread into very thin slices. Heat half of the milk and pour over the bread. Let rest for a few minutes. Melt 2 Tbs butter in a skillet and add the moist bread. Brown lightly, turning frequently. Mix the remaining milk with the eggs and salt. Pour over the bread. Keep turning until the eggs begin to curdle. Form the bread into a cake and add the remaining butter. Cover the pan and fry until the crust is golden brown. Place on a hot platter and serve with fruit preserves or salad.

## Omelette Jurassienne

*6-8 eggs, 1 dl milk, salt, pepper, 50 g (2 oz) lean diced*
*bacon, 1 chopped onion, 2 Tbs butter, 2 potatoes*
*boiled in their jackets, 150 g (5 oz) Gruyère cheese*

Beat the eggs with the milk and season with salt and pepper. Sauté the onions and bacon in a large frying pan with butter. Peel and dice the potatoes, add to the bacon. When they start to change color, pour in the eggs. Sprinkle with the finely cubed cheese. Cook through on both sides, then fold the omelet over and slide on to a warm plate.

Note: Sometimes other cooked vegetables such as carrots, peas or cauliflower florets are added in addition to the potatoes. Or the omelet is topped with chopped parsley or chives.

83

# Cheese Fondue
## Basic Recipe

*600 g (21 oz) shredded cheese (¹/₂ Gruyère, ¹/₂ Emmentaler), 1 garlic clove, 3 dl (1¹/₄ C) dry white wine, 3 tsp cornstarch, 3 small glasses kirsch, ground pepper, nutmeg*

Rub a heavy saucepan or heat proof clay fondue pot (Caquelon) with the split garlic clove. Dissolve the cornstarch in the kirsch.

Put the cheese and wine into the pan and slowly bring to a boil, stirring constantly. When the cheese is completly melted, add the kirsch and cornstarch mixture, stirring vigourously. Continue to cook. Season with pepper and nutmeg. Serve over an alcohol lamp. The cooking should continue on low heat. Stir constantly with small pieces of bread speared on a fondue fork.

There are several varieties of fondue:

In the canton of Vaud, fondue is prepared with Gruyère cheese only, but at varying stages of ripeness. Sometimes it is mixed with cheese from the Jura.

In the canton of Fribourg, fondue is either served Moité-Moité (half/half), meaning 300 g (10¹/₂ oz) Fribourg Vacherin and 300 g (10¹/₂ oz) Gruyère, or only with Vacherin but without wine. The latter version calls for a very ripe Vacherin. The cheese is melted at low heat with 1 dl (¹/₃ C) hot water. The fondue should not boil. It is served in a fondue pot over a candle (not alcohol-)burner.

In the Jura, the fondue is made up of at ¹/₂ Jura cheese and enhanced with 1-2 shallots per person. The shallots are eaten last.

In Geneva three kinds of cheese are used: Gruyère, Emmentaler and a Vaudois cheese. Then, sautéed chopped morels (fresh or dried and pre-soaked) or diced tomatoes are added.

Fondue is usually eaten with bite-sized pieces of crusty bread speared on a fondue fork. One can also, however, use small potatoes or potato pieces. Fondue aficionados dunk their bread in kirsch before dipping it into the cheese. And don't forget: whoever loses his bread in the pan must pay for a round of beer or a bottle of wine. If it happens to a lady she must kiss the man sitting next to her. On the whole, however, the former is more popular.

# Fotzelschnitten
## (Fried Bread Slices)

*2 dl (³/₄ C) milk, 4 eggs, salt, nutmeg, 8 stale slices*
*brown bread, 3 Tbs butter*

Heat the milk in a small saucepan. Beat the eggs with salt and a bit of nutmeg. Stick the bread slices on a fork and dip first in the milk and then in the eggs. Melt a part of the butter. Add 2-3 slices of bread and fry until golden brown on both sides. Put in a warm place and proceed in the same way with the rest of the bread. Serve with plum jam, apple sauce or salad.

# Ramequins

*250 g (9 oz) day-old brown bread, ¹/₄ L (1 C) milk,*
*70 g (2¹/₂ oz) butter, 4 eggs, salt, nutmeg, 150 g (5 oz)*
*grated Gruyère cheese*

Cut the crust off the bread and cut into pieces. Pour the milk in a bowl and add the bread. Soak until all the liquid is absorbed. Melt 1 Tbs butter in a saucepan and add the bread mixture. Stir over moderate heat until the mass begins to separate from the pan. Whip the rest of the butter until it is creamy and combine with the beaten egg yolk, herbs and cheese. Add to the bread. Whip the egg white until stiff and stir into the bread/cheese mixture. Spread into a well greased baking dish and bake in a 200° C (390° F) preheated oven for 15-20 minutes. Serve hot.

# Gruyère Cheese Cake

*For a round 24 cm (9 in) pan: 300 g (10½ oz) cheese-cake crust, 5 dl (2 C) double cream, 1 dl (⅓ C) milk, 1 Tbs flour, 2 egg yolks, 4 eggs, 250 g (9 oz) Gruyère cheese, salt, pepper, nutmeg, butter for the pan*

Beat the cream with the egg yolks and the 4 whole eggs. Mix the milk and flour and add to the egg mixture. Stir well. Season with salt, pepper and nutmeg. Roll out the dough 3 mm (1/10 in) thick and place in a lightly greased cake pan. Prick several times with a fork. Grate the cheese onto the dough. Pour in the egg mixture and bake at 200° C (390° F) for 40 minutes. The surface of the cake should be light brown. Serve with a bowl of tossed salad.

# Chäshappech
# (Appenzell Cheese Pastries)

*4 dl (1½ C) milk, 300 g (10½ oz) Appenzeller cheese, 500 g (1 lb) flour, 1 tsp baking-powder, 3½ dl (1⅓ C) light beer, 8 eggs, fat for deep-frying*

Heat the milk. Stir in the thinly sliced cheese until it melts. Let cool. Sift the flour and baking-powder into a bowl. Add the beer and stir into a smooth batter. Add to the cheese/milk mixture. Beat the eggs and add to the batter. Mix well. The batter should now be somewhat thicker than pancake batter.
Let stand for 1 hour. Swirl into the hot fat (170° C/338° F) and deep-fry until light yellow in color.
Served with plenty of salad, this is a full meal. It also tastes good as a snack with a glass of wine or beer.

# Cheese Salad

*350 g (12 oz) Appenzeller cheese, 1 large onion, 1 bouquet chives, 4 Tbs oil, 2 Tbs vinegar, salt, pepper*

Finely slice the cheese and onion and cut the chives diagonally. Place in a bowl and mix together. Prepare a salad dressing with the oil, vinegar, salt and pepper. Pour over the cheese and mix. Let draw. Serve with crunchy bread.

# Basle Cheese Toast

*8 slices white bread (French or Italian), 50 g (4 Tbs)*
*butter, 4 onions, 250 g (9 oz) Gruyère cheese, ground*
*pepper*

Spread the bread with butter and place with the buttered side facing down, in a casserole. Chop the onions and sauté in the remaining butter until light yellow in color. Spread over the bread slices. Place in a 230° C (450° F) preheated oven and bake until the cheese melts. Sprinkle with freshly ground pepper and serve at once. Serve with salad.

# Bernese Cheese Toast

*8 thin slices French or Italian white bread, 2 Tbs*
*butter, 1 dl (⅓ C) milk, 250 g (9 oz) grated Gruyère*
*cheese, 2 egg yolks, 1 Tbs kirsch, 2 egg whites, salt,*
*pepper, nutmeg*

Spread the bread on one side with butter. Place buttered side down in a soufflé dish or small baking dishes. Trickle a small amount of milk over the bread. Combine cheese, egg yolks, remaining milk and kirsch. Mix together well. Whip the egg whites until stiff and fold into the egg and cheese mixture. Spread on the bread. Bake at 220° C (428° F) until the cheese melts and the toast turns golden.

# Deep-Fried Open Cheese Sandwiches

*400 g (14 oz) grated hard cheese (Gruyère), 2 eggs,*
*2 garlic cloves, 1 Tbs kirsch, 1 tsp baking-powder,*
*2 Tbs flour, salt, pepper, nutmeg, 8-12 slices white*
*bread (French or Italien), 1 egg white, fat for deep-*
*frying*

Combine cheese, beaten eggs, pressed garlic and kirsch. Sift the baking-powder and flour into a bowl. Add cheese mixture and work into a dough. Spread one side of the bread slices with the lightly whipped egg white and cover thickly with the cheese mixture. The spread should be so thick that the bread looks like a half circle. Flatten it out using a knife. Plunge into deep fat (180° C/356° F) until golden brown. Serve immediately with plenty of green salad.

# Geneva Cheese Soufflé

*2 Tbs butter, 4 Tbs flour, ¼ L (1 C) milk, salt, pep-*
*per, 4 egg whites, 160 g (5½ oz) grated Gruyère*
*cheese, 4 egg yolks, butter for the soufflé dish*

Grease a high soufflé dish or several small cocotte dishes with butter.
Preheat the oven to 190° C (375° F). Sift the flour. Melt the butter
and blend with the flour over low heat. Stir until the mixture becomes foamy, then stir in the cold milk. Season with salt and pepper
and cook into a thick sauce. Remove from heat. Stir in the cheese
and beaten eggs. Beat the egg whites until stiff and fold into the
cheese mixture. Pour into the soufflé baking dishes. They should not
be any more than ¾ full. Place in the hot oven. Bake for 20 minutes
at 190° C (375° F), then for another 10 minutes at 230° C (450° F).
The small baking dishes only take 20 minutes altogether. Do not
open the oven door before the soufflé is done. Serve immediately,
before it collapses.

# Malakoffs
# (Cheese Fritters)

This speciality with the Russian name is said to be a remnant from
the Swiss mercenaries which brought it back with them from Russia.
The best Malakoffs are found in the region of Nyon.

*300 g (10½ oz) Gruyère cheese, 1 dl (⅓ C) white*
*wine, pepper out of a mill, 150 g (1¼ C) flour, 2 dl*
*(¾ C) white wine for the dough, salt, 1 Tbs oil, 2 egg*
*whites, fat for deep-frying*

Cut the cheese into finger-sized sticks. Place in a bowl and sprinkle
with a generous amount of freshly ground pepper. Add the wine and
let draw for 1-2 hours. For the fritter batter sift the flour into a bowl,
add the wine and mix into a smooth dough. It should not be too run-
ny. Season with salt and rest for 1 hour.
Whip the egg whites until stiff and fold into the batter along with the
oil. Drain the cheese sticks well. Dust with flour and dip into the batter. Fry in deep fat or oil (190° C/375° F) until golden brown.
Note: Instead of white wine, you may use water or milk in the preparation of the fritter batter.

# Raclette

Raclette is the classical Valais recipe. It is served in most restaurants in this area.

One says that raclette was invented by accident by a group of wine-growers who built a fire because they were cold. Somehow a piece of cheese fell into the fire and melted. They then spread the melted cheese on their bread and loved it.

In preparing raclette, it is very important that you use the right kind of cheese.

*Per person: 200-250 g (7-9 oz) raclette cheese or any meltable semi-hard cheese, several small, hot, un-peeled boiled potatoes, cornichons, pickles, mari-nated onions, mixed pickles, pepper from a mill*

It is traditional in preparing raclette to place ½ of a wheel of cheese in front of an open fire or any other strong source of heat. There are special raclette ovens for this purpose. As soon as the cheese surface melts, it is sluffed off with a large knife onto a warm plate. Sprinkle with some freshly ground pepper, take a hot potato and some onions and pickles and eat immediately. The cheese must not be allowed to cool, so do not wait until everyone has been served; eat one after the other.

Nowadays the cheese is often simply cut into 3 mm (¹/₁₀ in) thick slices, then placed in a small skillet and melted in the oven or under the grill. You can also buy special table grills with mini skillets in which you place the cheese to be melted.

Served with a chilled, dry white wine, a raclette dinner is always fun to share with a group of friends.

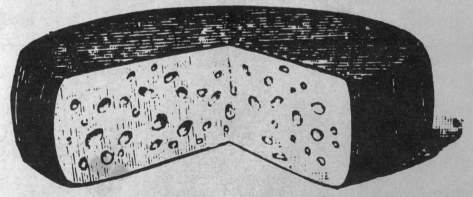

89

# Notes and more recipes

# Notes and more recipes

fig. 8

Families with many children very often eat a sweet evening meal.
Usually this are dishes made according to old traditional recipes. In
the winter they are usually made up of eggs, stale bread and maybe
apples. In the summer they include fresh fruit such as cherries and
plums.

Healthfood...

## Birchermüesli

No Swiss cookbook is complete without a real Birchermüesli. The
original recipe, however, only contains oats, water, condensed milk,
lemon juice, nuts and apples. Following is a very tasty variation.

*6 Tbs rolled oats, 3 dl (1¼ C) milk, juice of
1-2 lemons, 1 apple, 1 banana, 1 orange, 6 Tbs
ground nuts, 200 g (7 oz) berries or other fruits*

Mix the oats with the milk and sugar. Wash the apple and grate into
the oat mixture. Add lemon juice and stir well to prevent discolor-
ation of the apple. Slice the banana. Peel, halve and pit the orange
and cut into thin slices. Cut the berries or other fruit into small pieces.
Add all fruit to the oat mixture and stir. Top with ground nuts before
serving.
Note: Garnish with whipped cream as desired. In Dr. Bircher's original recipe, only apples are used and instead of milk, a half-and-half
water and condensed milk mixture.

94

# Cholermues
## (A Sweet Pancake)

*80 g (³/₄ C) flour, 4 eggs, 2¹/₂ dl (1 C) milk, 2 Tbs sug-*
*ar, 1 pinch salt, 2 Tbs butter, cinnamon sugar made*
*from 4 Tbs sugar and 1 tsp cinnamon*

Sift the flour into a bowl. Add the beaten eggs, milk, sugar and salt
and mix into a smooth dough. Let rest for 1 hour. If the dough is too
thick, dilute it with some milk. Heat the butter in a skillet. Pour in
the batter and make a large pancake. When the underside is golden
brown, cut the pancake into pieces with a spatula. Cook until all the
pieces are lightly browned. Serve sprinkled with cinnamon sugar,
accompanied by sautéed apple or pear slices.
Note: The pancake is especially delicate when the batter is prepared
with cream instead of milk or a half-and-half mixture.

# Conterser Bock
## (A Baked Egg Delight)

*1 hard-cooked egg, 4 eggs, 200 g (1²/₃ C) flour, 2¹/₂ dl*
*(1 C) milk, 1 pinch salt, 1 Tbs oil, fat for deep-frying*
*For the sauce: 2 dl (³/₄ C) water, 125 g (¹/₂ C 2 Tbs)*
*sugar, 2 cloves, 1 cinnamon stick, 1 slice lemon, ¹/₂ L*
*(2 C) red wine*

Beat the eggs with the milk. Add sifted flour and salt. Work into a
thick pancake dough. Let stand a while before cooking. Mix in the
oil. Dip in the hard boiled egg (without the shell). The batter should
stick to the egg. Deep-fry in hot fat until it turns light brown. Remove, dip into the batter a second time and deep-fry again. Repeat
this process until the egg reaches the desired size.
For the sauce, cook all the given ingredients except the wine. Pour in
the wine. Reheat the sauce, but do not boil.
To serve, cut the "Bock" into 4 or 8 uniform slices. Cover with the
wine sauce and serve immediately.
Note: If children will be eating also, it is advisable to serve them
apple instead of red wine sauce.

## Fastenkutteln
## (Lenten Tripe)

*150 g (1¼ C) flour, 2½-3 dl (1-1¼ C) milk, 1 pinch*
*salt, 4 eggs, 2 Tbs butter, 4 apples, 1 Tbs sugar, 1 Tbs*
*lemon juice, butter for baking dish*
*Vanilla sauce: 2 egg yolks, 2 Tbs sugar, 4 dl (1½ C)*
*milk, 1 vanilla bean, 1 Tbs potato flour*

Combine flour, milk and salt into a smooth dough. Beat the eggs and add to the dough. Let stand for 1 hour. Make pancakes by frying the batter in butter.

For the sauce, beat egg yolks and sugar. Bring the milk (save a few spoonfuls) and slit vanilla bean to a boil. Remove from heat and let cool for a few minutes. Mix the remaining milk with the potato flour and add to the egg/sugar mixture. Return all ingredients to saucepan and scald. Let cool, stirring constantly.

Grate the apples and immediately mix with lemon juice and sugar. Roll up the pancakes and cut into strips. Place in alternate layers in a lightly greased, ovenproof baking dish. Pour over the vanilla sauce and bake in a 200° C (390° F) preheated oven for 20 minutes.

Note: This dish may also be prepared in a salty version, whereby the apples are replaced with grated cheese, and the vanilla sauce with a simple sauce made of milk and eggs.

## Cherry Soup

*800 g (1½ lbs) unpitted cherries, 3 Tbs sugar, 3½ dl*
*(1⅓ C) milk, 170 g (1½ C) flour*

Wash the cherries. Place in a bowl and cover with sugar. Stirring constantly, brown the flour in a large, dry saucepan. Let cool. Place in a large bowl. Add the cold milk and stir into a smooth, thin paste. Blend in the cherries and juice. Let cool in the refrigerator for 1-2 hours. Before serving, add a bit of milk. The soup should not be too thick. Serve cold.

# Öpfelbröisi
## (Apple Rösti)

*350 g (12 oz) day-old bread (French or Italian),*
*4 Tbs butter, 500 g (18 oz) apples, 3 Tbs sugar, 3 Tbs*
*raisins, 3 Tbs sugar, 1 tsp cinnamon*

Cut the bread into thin slices. Melt the butter in a skillet. Add the bread and brown lightly on all sides. Peel and core the apples. Cut into thin slices and add to the bread. Add 3 Tbs sugar and stir. Cover the pan, reduce the heat and cook until a light crust forms on the underside. Meanwhile mix the remaining sugar with the cinnamon. Flip the apple rösti onto a large plate and sprinkle with cinnamon sugar. Serve hot, with white coffee or cold milk.

# Matafan

*8 slices white bread, 7¹/₂ dl (3 C) milk, 150 g (1¹/₄ C)*
*flour, 3 eggs, salt, 3 Tbs sugar, 1 Tbs butter, butter for*
*the cookie sheet, sugar*

Place the bread in a dish. Pour in half of the heated milk. Let stand for a few minutes. Sift the flour into a bowl and mix with the beaten eggs and the remaining milk. Stir into a dough. Add salt, sugar and lukewarm, melted butter. Grease a cookie sheet with butter and place the bread slices on it. They should be close together. Pour over the dough and dot with butter. Bake in a 180° C (356° F) preheated oven for 25-30 minutes. You should get a flat, golden cake. Cut while still warm and sprinkle with sugar. Serve with apple sauce or fruit compote.

# Plattenmüesli

*5 dl (2 C) milk, 6 eggs, 2 Tbs sugar, 1 pinch salt,*
*½ tsp grated lemon rind, butter, confectioners' sugar*

Grease a flat, ovenproof dish with butter. Combine all remaining above ingredients and pour into the dish. Cover with aluminum foil and bake for 15-20 minutes in a 170° C (338° F) preheated oven. Do not let it dry out. Sprinkle with confectioners' sugar and serve immediately.

Note: For variety you may choose to pour the egg mixture into 4 greased molds. This will reduce the baking time to 10-12 minutes.

# Plain in Padella
# (Bread Rösti)

*4 stale Kaiser rolls, 2 Tbs butter, 2 Tbs raisins, 1 tsp*
*cinnamon, 3 Tbs sugar, 3 dl (1¼ C) milk, 4 eggs*

Cut rolls into small cubes and sauté in butter. Heat the milk and add to it the raisins and sugar. Pour this mixture over the rolls. Beat the eggs and pour over the roll mixture. Fry, until the mass comes away from the pan. Turn and fry the other side until golden brown.

# Plum Rösti

*500 g (18 oz) plums, 4 Tbs butter, 4 Tbs sugar, 250 g*
*(9 oz) day-old bread (French or Italian), sugar and*
*cinnamon*

Halve and pit the plums. Heat 1 Tbs butter. Sauté the plums in the butter with 1 Tbs sugar. Add 1½ dl (½ C) water. Cover and simmer for 2-3 minutes. Cut the bread into thin slices. Brown lightly in a large skillet with the remaining butter. Add the plums without juice and the rest of the butter. Simmer, turning frequently. Gradually add the plum juice. Simmer until the liquid is almost completely reduced. Serve hot. Sprinkle with cinnamon sugar as desired.

# Notes and more recipes

fig · 9

# Cereals and Pasta

The Swiss love pasta. Pasta came to Switzerland from Italy and was soon a staple in the mountain regions because it could be stored for long periods of time, and mixed with milk, cream and cheese, made a delicious meal. From these days stems the popular "Älplermagronen", a simple mountain meal for which city dwellers especially are willing to drive very long distances.

Rice also came to Switzerland from the south. In the Ticino, risotto and polenta are the most popular dishes. Corn dishes are also often found in Graubünden and the Rhine valley regions.

## Älplermagronen

This is how the Älplermagronen are prepared in the canton of Unterwalden. In Uri, the potatoes are left out.

> *250 g (9 oz) potatoes, salt, 250 g (9 oz) straight, hollow noodles, 200 g (7 oz) grated cheese, 2 dl (¾ C) cream, 3 Tbs butter, 2 large onions*

Peel and dice the potatoes. Boil in salted water. Add the noodles shortly before the potatotes are done (read the directions on the package first). The potatoes should be soft. Drain and arrange in alternate layers with the cheese in a deep baking dish. Pour in the cream and place in the hot oven for a few minutes until the cheese melts. Meanwhile, melt the butter in a skillet. Slice the onions and sauté until they turn light brown. Spread over the noodles and potatoes.

Serve with apple purée or salad.

# Chnöpfli

The Glarner Chnöpfli are prepared with Schabzieger, an interesting herb cheese. This cheese is available in a conical shape and must be grated before using it for cooking.

*500 g (18 oz) fresh spinach (or 250 g / 9 oz frozen spinach), 1 dl (⅓ C) milk, 4 eggs, 400 g (3⅓ C) flour, 50 g (2 oz) grated cheese, salt, 2 Tbs fresh butter*

Wash the spinach and remove any damaged leaves. Steam until limp in a deep saucepan. Drain well and finely chop (frozen spinach must of course be thawed). Beat the milk with 1 dl (⅓ C) water and the eggs. Sift in the flour. Add the spinach and half of the grated cheese. Add some salt. If necessary, add some more water, but the dough must be relatively firm. Let rest for 1 hour.
Rub the dough in portions through a sieve into a large pot of boiling salted water. When the dough bits rise to the surface they are done. Remove with a colander and drain. Before serving, melt some butter in a frying pan and swish the "Chnöpfli" in, without letting them brown.

# Pasta con Patate
## (Pasta with potatoes)

The poor population of the Ticino valleys traditionally mixed pasta with the cheaper potatoes. This is an interesting and very tasty combination thanks to the cheese and garlic added.

*250 g (9 oz) pasta, salt, pepper, 3 unpeeled, boiled potatoes, 3 Tbs butter, 3 garlic cloves, 50 g (2 oz) grated cheese*

Boil the noodles in generously salted water until tender. Peel and dice potatoes and fry in butter until golden brown. Finely chop the garlic and add to the potatoes. Sauté briefly. Drain noodles well and mix into the potatoes. Season to taste with salt and pepper. Serve topped with grated cheese.

## Polenta Ticino Style

Authentic polenta requires a lot of patience because it needs to be conscientiously stirred.

In the Ticino, polenta is served in a basket covered with a linen cloth and cut with a string.

In the past, milk was poured over the polenta and it was eaten like that without any accompaniment.

*1½ L (1½ qts) water, salt, 300 g (1¼ C) cornmeal*

Bring the water and salt to a boil. Gradually stir in the cornmeal. Reduce heat and cook, stirring constantly, until a crust begins to form around the edges. The polenta is done after cooking for 30-40 minutes. Add a piece of butter as desired before serving.

Note: You may choose to use a precooked cornmeal mush which is cooked in 2 minutes. Slowly cooked polenta does, however, taste better. Leftover polenta can be sliced, fried in butter and served as an accompaniment with another dish.

## Türkenribel
## (A Corn Dish)

*300 g (10½ oz) cornmeal, salt, 2 day-old boiled po-*
*tatoes in their jackets, 100 g (3½ oz) butter*

Pour the cornmeal in a bowl and add 3 dl (1¼ C) boiling salted water. Peel and finely grate the potatoes. Stir into what is now cornmeal mush. Melt 3 Tbs butter in a saucepan and add the cornmeal mixture. Turn constantly at low heat until the mass forms into small lumps. From time to time add a bit more butter. (This is a rather time-consuming procedure.) Proceed this way until the whole mass in crumbly. Dot with butter and serve.

Türkenribel is excellent with a meat and sauce dish, but it also tastes great on its own, served with a salad.

Note: Many people top this dish with cracklings and onion rings.

*I could eat this every day*

## Risotto ai Funghi
## (Rice with Mushrooms)

Every year on the occasion of the carnival, the larger towns of the Ticino region serve risotto out of a large kettle on the main square of the town. This is called the "Risotto in piazza". Large and small, tourists and all, are welcome to participate in the fun.

> *20 g (1½ Tbs) dried mushrooms, ½ L (2 C) bouillon, 4 Tbs butter, 1 large onion, ½ L (2 C) short or medium grain rice, 2 dl (¾ C) red wine, salt, pepper, 50 g (2 oz) freshly grated cheese, 30 g (2 Tbs) fresh butter*

Soak the mushrooms in ½ L (2 C) bouillon for 30 minutes. In a heavy pan, heat butter. Chop onions and sauté until translucent. Add the rice. Pour in wine and simmer until wine evaporates. Add bouillon with mushrooms. Season with salt and a generous amount of pepper. Cook at low heat for 18 minutes occasionally adding bouillon. Mix in grated cheese and butter and serve immediately.

It is advisable to let your guests wait for the risotto rather than the other way around. Be sure to plan your preparation keeping in mind that it must be served immediately. In the southern (Ticino) region of Switzerland risotto is also served in soup bowls as an appetizer. You may also choose to replace the mushrooms with saffron, making it similar to Risotto Milanese, which is frequently served as an accompaniement to meat dishes.

The basis of these popular specialities is any rich pie dough or a Pâte Brisée. The pie shell is then filled with vegetables, onions, bacon or any local produce which is often covered with a mixture of eggs, milk and sometimes cheese. These spicy pies are served as a main meal with a fresh tossed green salad.

## Pâte Brisée
### Basic recipe

*250 g (9 oz) flour, 125 g (4¹/₂ oz) butter, ¹/₂ tsp salt*

Sift the flour onto a flat surface. Rub the flour and small pieces of butter together with your fingers until the mixture has a fine, crumbly consistency. Make a well and pour in 1 dl (¹/₃ C) salted water. Quickly work into a dough, moving from the inside to the other edge. If necessary, add 1-2 tablespoons more water. Warning: Do not knead the dough, otherwise it will become tough and sticky. Prepare this dough the night before you plan to use it or let it stand in a cool place for at·least 2-3 hours.

## Spinach Pie

*For a round 24 cm (9 in) pie pan: 400 g (14 oz) Pâte Brisée (see above), 50 g (2 oz) diced lean bacon (small pieces), 1 Tbs butter, 500 g (18 oz) cooked spinach leaves, 1 onion, salt, pepper, 1 Tbs flour, 2 dl (³/₄ C) cream, 2 eggs, nutmeg*

Fry the bacon in a heavy saucepan until golden. Remove. Now melt the butter and add the well drained coarsely chopped spinach and finely chopped onions. Sauté for 2-3 minutes. Season with salt, pepper and nutmeg, let cool. Mix well, flour, eggs and cream. Roll out the dough 2 mm (¹/₁₀ in) thick and place in the pie pan. Prick with a fork several times and sprinkle with the bacon. Spread with the spinach mixture and pour over the egg/flour mixture. Bake in a preheated 220° C (428° F) oven for 40-50 minutes.

108

# Original Lucerne Chügeli Pastry

## 6-8 servings

*600-700 g (1½ lbs) Pâte Brisée (see page 108), 1 small,*
*round breakfast roll, 2 egg yolks*
*For the filling: 250 g (9 oz) pork, 250 g (9 oz) veal,*
*140 g (5 oz) each, professionally prepared ground*
*pork and veal, 4 Tbs butter, 1 onion, 2 dl (¾ C) white*
*wine, 1 apple, coriander, marjoram, 2 Tbs flour, 3 dl*
*(1¼ C) milk, 50 g (1¾ oz) grapes, 1 Tbs pear liqueur*
*or kirsch, 250 g (9 oz) mushrooms, salt, pepper,*
*nutmeg, 2 Tbs cream, 3 dl (1¼ C) bouillon, 1 Tbs*
*chopped almonds*

The "pastry house" must be formed and baked before beginning
with the preparation of the filling:
Roll out the dough to 4 mm (⅕ in) thickness. With a biscuit cutter,
cut out two circles: one smaller one, 24 cm (9 in) in diameter and one
large one, 32 cm (13 in) in diameter. Place the smaller one on a large
cake pan rinsed with cold water. Prick several times with a fork.
Wrap the roll in as much tissue paper as necessary to form a ball of
37-38 cm (15 in) in circumference. Place this ball in the middle of
the dough on the cake pan. Moisten the edges with water and carefully cover the ball with larger piece of dough. Pinch the edges firmly
together. Knead the leftover dough and cut it into 3 cm (1 in) by
6 mm (¼ in) strips. Brush the "pastry house" with the beaten egg
yolk. Place four strips of dough crosswise over the ball. Wrap two
more strips around the ball. Place another strip of dough around the
bottom to cover up the loose ends. Decorate the pastry with stars,
hearts and crescents made from the remaining bits of dough; and top
with a rosette. Brush again with egg yolk and bake for 40 minutes in
a preheated 180° C (356° F) oven.
After 25 minutes, cover with aluminum foil. Remove from oven and
let stand for 5 minutes. Using a sharp knife, separate the upper half
and carefully remove the paper ball as long as the dough is still lukewarm and soft. (Perhaps it is also possible to order one of these "pastry houses" from your local bakery.)
For the filling, brown the diced meat in 1 Tbs butter. Chop the onion
and add it to the meat. Pour in ½ dl (2 Tbs) white wine and simmer
for 10 minutes. Peel the apple and grate it over the onions and meat.

Soak the grapes in pear schnaps or kirsch. Combine the ground veal and pork, season with coriander and marjoram and form into little balls. Let draw in the bouillon for 10 minutes. For the sauce, melt the flour in 2 Tbs butter and cover with the milk and remaining wine. Add the gravy from the meat and the grapes in schnaps or kirsch. Simmer gently for 20 minutes. Clean the mushrooms and slice them into 4 parts. Sauté in the remaining butter, season with salt and pepper. Add the meat, mushrooms and meat balls to the sauce. Reheat, season and if necessary dilute with some cream or bouillon. Place the hot filling into the pastry. Sprinkle with dry roasted almonds and cover with the top.

## Schaffuser Bölletünne
## (Onion Pie)

*For a round 24 cm (9 in) pie pan: 300 g (10½ oz) Pâte Brisée (see page 108) or Basic Pie Dough, 800 g (2 lbs) onions, 50 g (1¾ oz) lean, diced bacon, 2 Tbs butter, 2 eggs, 1 Tbs cornstarch, 2 dl (¾ C) sour cream, salt, pepper, nutmeg, ½ tsp caraway seeds, butter flakes*

Preheat oven to 230° C (450° F).
Roll out the dough until it is about 4 mm (⅕ in) thick. Grease the pie pan with butter and line with the dough. Prick several times with a fork. Thinly slice the onions. In a heavy saucepan melt the butter and add the onions and bacon. Stir and cook for five minutes. Spread evenly over the dough. Blend the eggs with the cornstarch and sour cream. Season with salt, pepper, nutmeg and caraway seeds and pour over the onions. Dot with flakes of butter and place in the preheated oven for 40 minutes. If necessary, cover with aluminum foil towards the end of the baking time.
Note: Instead of sour cream, you may use a half cream/half milk mixture.

# Potato Pie

*For a round 24 cm (9 in) pie pan: 5 large potatoes,*
*200 g (7 oz) bacon, 2 onions, 2 eggs, ¼ L (1 C)*
*cream, salt, nutmeg, 300 g (10½ oz) Basic Pie*
*Dough, butter to grease the pan*

Boil the unpeeled potatoes until soft. Let cool and peel. Cut the
bacon into cubes or strips. Fry at low heat in a skillet. Add the
chopped onions and sauté for 10 minutes. Grate the potatoes over
the onions and bacon and mix together. Mix the eggs with the cream,
season with salt and nutmeg and add to the potatoes. Roll out the
dough 3 mm (¹/₁₀ in) thick and place in the greased pie pan. Prick several times with a fork. Spread with the filling and place in a preheated 220° C (428° F) oven. Bake until the crust is brown.
Note: Enhance the filling with some grated cheese, chopped parsley
or steamed leek as desired.

# Asparagus Pie

*For a round 24 cm (9 in) pie pan: 300 g (10½ oz)*
*Pâte Brisée (see page 108), butter for the pan, 1 kg*
*(2.2 lbs) medium-sized, white asparagus, 2 Tbs but-*
*ter, 2½ dl (1 C) cream, 1 egg, salt, pepper, nutmeg,*
*1 dash sugar, 1 tsp butter*

Roll out the dough 3 mm (¹/₁₀ in) thick. Place in the greased pan and
prick several times with a fork. Cover with a piece of aluminum foil.
Weigh down the foil with cherry stones or beans. Bake (blind) in a
200° C (390° F) preheated oven.
Cut the stalks in half (use the bottom halves for a soup). Peel from
the tips down. Cook in salted water with dash of sugar and tsp butter
until tender. Drain and place on a paper towel. Melt the remaining
butter in a saucepan. Add the asparagus tips and sauté for 2-3 minutes. Remove and arrange in the pie shell. Mix the cream and egg,
season with salt, pepper and nutmeg and pour over the asparagus.
Bake the pie in a 220° C (428° F) oven for another 10-15 minutes.
Serve hot.

111

# Cheese and Bacon Pie

*400 g (14 oz) Pâte Brisée (see page 108), butter for*
*the pan, 200 g (7 oz) lean bacon slices, 250 g (9 oz)*
*grated cheese, 2 eggs, 1 tsp oil, 1 dl (¹/₃ C) white wine,*
*1 tsp caraway*

Roll out the dough 3 mm (¹/₁₀ in) thick and place in a greased pie pan.
Prick dough with a fork. Cut the bacon into thin strips and distribute
evenly over the dough. Sprinkle with the cheese. Beat the eggs with
oil and wine and pour over the bacon. Sprinkle with caraway seeds
and bake for 30 minutes in a 200° C (390° F) preheated oven.
Note: Check on the pie after 5-10 minutes. If the dough is blistered,
prick it with a sharp knife.

# Tomato Pie

*300 g (10¹/₂ oz) Pâte Brisée (see page 108), 2-3 Tbs*
*bread crumbs, 750 g (1¹/₂ lbs) tomatoes, 150 g (5 oz)*
*diced bacon, 150 g (5 oz) semi-hard cheese, 3 eggs,*
*2¹/₂ dl (1 C) cream, salt, pepper, nutmeg, 2 Tbs*
*chopped parsley*

Rinse a large pie pan with cold water. Line with the 3 mm (¹/₁₀ in)
thick dough. Prick the dough generously and sprinkle with the bread
crumbs. Cut the tomatoes into slices. Seed lightly. Arrange in layers,
along with the lightly fried bacon cubes in the pie shell. Grate or
thinly slice the cheese and spread over the tomatoes. Mix eggs and
cream and season with salt, pepper and nutmeg. Pour over the tomatoes. Bake in a preheated 180° C (356° F) oven for 40 minutes.
Before serving, sprinkle with the finely chopped parsley.

# Sèche au Lard
# (Bacon Pie)

*500 g (1 lb) flour, 250 g (9 oz) pork lard, ¹/₂ tsp salt,*
*fat to grease the pan, 300 g (10¹/₂ oz) lean bacon,*
*butter flakes*

Work the flour into the lard with the tips of your fingers until it has a
crumbly consistency. Add the salt and gradually ¹/₂-1 dl (2-4 Tbs)

water. Punch the dough down several times, than form it into a ball. It should be firm but smooth. Let cool for 2 hours.

Roll the dough out on a floured surface as thin as possible. Spread it onto a greased baking sheet. Prick several times with a fork and cover with a layer of thinly sliced bacon. Dot the bacon with a few flakes of butter. Bake 15-20 minutes in a preheated 200° C (425° F) oven until light brown. Cut into squares and serve.

## Meat Pie

*For the dough: 220 g (2 C) flour, 175 g (6 oz) butter, ½ dl (2 Tbs) milk, 1 egg yolk, some salt*
*For the filling: 250 g (9 oz) ground pork, 250 g (9 oz) ground veal, 1 Tbs butter, 1 breakfast roll, ½ dl (2 Tbs) milk, 100 g (3½ oz) lean bacon cubes, 1 large onion, ½ dl (2 Tbs) red wine, ½ dl (2 Tbs) brown sauce, ½ dl (2 Tbs) cream, salt, paprika, marjoram, butter to grease the pan, 1 egg yolk*

In a bowl, work the butter into the flour. Beat the egg yolk and heat the milk. Add both, together with some salt, to the butter and flour mixture and mix into a smooth dough. Cover and let cool for 1 hour. Heat some butter in a pan and brown the meat. Add the bacon cubes and the chopped onion and sauté for 5 minutes. Cut the roll in cubes and cover with milk. Let soak for a few minutes. Drain the rolls, put them through a sieve and add to the meat. Remove the meat mixture from the saucepan.

Add the red wine and brown sauce to the gravy and bring to a boil. Pour in the cream and let the sauce thicken for 2-3 minutes. Return the meat mixture to the pan and season to taste with salt, paprika and marjoram.

Roll out the dough and cut out a circle of 22 cm (8 in) circumference. Place on a cake pan greased with butter. Spread with the filling, leaving a free edge of 2 cm (¾ in). Moisten this edge with water or milk. Cut out a second circle 24 cm (9 in) in circumference. Place over the filling and firmly pinch the edges together. Prick the surface several times with a fork. Decorate with the leftover dough as desired. Brush with the egg yolk and place in a preheated 220° C (428° F) oven.

113

# Desserts

The Swiss love sweets. A delicate dessert has always been the way to crown a good meal, and thus many delicious specialities have been passed down from one generation to another. The traditional desserts are still the best, and it is gratifying to see that they are still popular with grownups and children alike.

## Apricot Flan

The Valais is the fruit orchard of Switzerland. From here stem many of the Swiss apricot and pear recipes.

*500 g (18 oz) apricots, butter for the pan, 3 Tbs*
*sugar, 4 eggs, 1 dash salt, 3 dl (1¼ C) milk or cream,*
*300 g (10½ oz) bakers' cheese, ½ tsp vanilla extract*

Halve and pit the apricots. Place, with the opening facing downward, in a greased, ovenproof baking dish. Sprinkle each layer of fruit with a bit of sugar. Beat the eggs with the remaining sugar, milk or cream, bakers' cheese and vanilla extract and pour over the apricots. Place the dish in a larger dish half-filled with water. Place in a 180° C (356° F) preheated oven and bake for approx. 20 minutes. The cream should curdle, but must not be dry.

## Prunes in Red Wine

*1 kg (2.2 lbs) dried prunes, 2 L (2 qts) red wine, 400 g*
*(2 C) sugar, 1 cinnamon stick, 1 lemon, 2 cloves,*
*1 bay leaf*

Place the prunes in a large bowl and cover with the wine. Let stand overnight. On the following day, pour the prunes and wine into a

116

skillet. Add sugar, cinnamon, thin slices of lemon rind, cloves and bay leaf. Bring to a boil. Pour into glass jars and seal. The prunes may be kept for at least two weeks.

Serve with whipped cream or vanilla ice cream.

## Brischtner Birä
## (Dried pears with whipped cream)

Dried fruit used to play a significant role in the diet of the Swiss mountain folk. This is an old recipe from Bristen, a town near the Gotthard mountain range.

*120 g (4 oz) dried pears (whole, meaty), 3 dl (1¹/₄ C) red wine, 4 Tbs sugar, ¹/₂ cinnamon stick or ¹/₂ tsp powder, 1 clove, 100 g (¹/₂ C) pear juice concentrate, 3 dl (1¹/₄ C) cream*

Soak the pears overnight in cold water. Bring the wine, sugar, cinnamon and clove to a boil. Add the pears, together with 1-2 dl (¹/₃-³/₄ C) liquid. Simmer gently for 30-40 minutes. Let cool. Remove the pears, reheat the liquid and add the pear concentrate. Cook until it has a syrupy consistency. Whip the cream and spread over a flat platter. Arrange the pears, stems upward on the whipped cream, and sprinkle with a tiny bit of the sauce. Serve the rest separately.

## Zabaione
## (Wine Custard)

*Per person: 1 egg yolk, 3 half egg shells white wine, ¹/₂ egg shell sugar*

In a bowl, beat egg yolks, wine and sugar. Place bowl in a saucepan half-filled with hot water. At low heat, beat the custard constantly with a wire beater until it doubles in bulk and begins to thicken. Carefull: Do not let the mixture boil! Serve immediately in sherbet glasses.

Note: Instead of white wine, you may use Marsala (or a half-and-half mixture). Zabaione is often served over scoop of vanilla ice cream. If you wish to serve it cold, add a bit of cornstarch at the beginning.

117

# Apple Must Custard

Here is a modest version of Zabaglione made from apple must called "Bauernsabayon" (Farmers' Zabaglione).

*3 egg yolks, 1 lemon, 80 g (1/3 C 1 Tbs) sugar, 1 tsp cornstarch, 5 dl (2 C) apple must (sweet cider), 2 dl (3/4 C) cream*

Mix the egg yolks, grated lemon rind, lemon juice, sugar, cornstarch and must in a saucepan. Scald the mixture over low heat while constantly shaking the pan. Shake for a few more minutes, but do not let it boil. Pour it into a bowl and let cool, stirring occasionally. Fold in the whipped cream before serving.

Note: Experienced cooks may enhance the custard by using 5 egg yolks instead of 3 and leave out the cornstarch.

# Apple Purée with Whipped Cream

*1 kg (2.2 lbs) apples, 1 dl (1/3 C) apple juice or water, juice and rind of 1/2 lemon, 1/2 cinnamon stick, 80-120 g (approx. 1/2 C) sugar, 1/4 L (1 C) cream*

Cut the peeled or unpeeled apples into quarters. Do not core. Place them in a saucepan and partly cover with apple juice or water. Add lemon juice and grated lemon rind and the cinnamon stick and bring to a boil. Cover and simmer until tender, stirring occasionally. Put through a ricer. Sweeten as desired with sugar. Whip the cream and spread over the lukewarm apple purée.

**For something different try:**

Apple Purée with Almonds and Hazelnuts: Brown 2 Tbs each chopped almonds and hazelnuts in a dry frying pan. Soak 1 Tbs raisins in rum or cognac. Pour nuts and raisins over the apple purée before serving. Sprinkle with cinnamon sugar. Serve separately with chilled whipped cream.

Apple Purée with Meringue: Pour the prepared apple purée in a greased ovenproof dish. Whip 4 egg whites until stiff and gradually stir in 150 g (3/4 C) sugar. Whip until very stiff. Put through a pastry tube and garnish the apple purée. Bake in a 200° C (390° F) oven until the egg white turns yellow.

Apple Purée with Caramel: Pour the apple purée into a decorative bowl. Brown 100 g (½ C) sugar without stirring, until it begins to foam. Add 1 Tbs water and stir. Pour over the apple purée.

## Apple Compote

*800 g (1½ lbs) apples, 3 Tbs sugar, 1 Tbs butter, 1 dl (⅓ C) apple must (sweet cider), 1 cinnamon stick, 2 lemon slices, 3 Tbs raisins*

Wash the apples. Cut into halves and core. Do not peel. Cut into slices. In a frying pan, lightly brown the sugar in the butter, stirring constantly. Add the apple slices. Shake the pan until the apples are coated with the sugar. Add cinnamon, lemon slices, raisins and the must. Stir until the sugar is dissolved. Cover and cook at low heat until tender. Serve lukewarm.

## Apples with Cream

*4 large firm apples, 6 Tbs sugar, 2 dl (¾ C) cream*

Pare, halve and core the apples. Place face up in an ovenproof dish and sprinkle with the 4 Tbs sugar. Pour the cream into the hollows allowing some of it to flow into the dish. Place in a 200° C (390° F) preheated oven. Remove after 10 minutes and sprinkle with the rest of the sugar. Return to the oven and continue to bake until the surface has as golden glaze (about 25-30 minutes). Check on the apples often to make sure that they do not fall apart.
Note: Pears may be prepared in the same way.

## Caramel Custard

*50 g (¹/₄ C) lump or loaf sugar, 1 lemon, 200 g (1 C)
coarse sugar, 1 L (1 qt) milk, 5 eggs, 2 dl (³/₄ C)
cream*

Rub down the sugar lumps on the washed lemon. Without stirring, melt the semolina sugar in a dry pan until light brown. Remove from heat and add milk and sugar lumps. Bring to a boil, stirring constantly. Beat the eggs until they are creamy. Pour the caramel milk into the eggs, while shaking the pan. Scald. Pour into a bowl. Sprinkle with sugar to prevent the formation of skin and let cool.
Before serving, whip the cream and carefully fold under the custard.

*Mikey loves it!*

## Chocolate Custard

Chocolate is a product which the world identifies with Switzerland. The first chocolate factories were built in 1819 and since then an endless amount of desserts and specialities are based on this main ingredient. Following is a dessert which you will find everywhere in the country.

*3 eggs, 50 g (¹/₄ C) sugar, 6 dl (2¹/₂ C) milk, 100 g
(3¹/₂ oz) semi-sweet chocolate, ¹/₂ Tbs cornstarch*

Beat the eggs with the sugar until foamy. Break the chocolate into pieces. Add to the milk and bring to a boil. Mix the remaining milk with the cornstarch and add to the chocolate milk. Bring to a boil. Stirring vigorously, add about half of the hot milk to the egg mixture. Remove saucepan from heat. Add the egg/chocolate mixture and return to hotplate. Stir the custard constantly over low heat (do not boil, otherwise the eggs will curdle) for another 2-3 minutes. Pour into custard cups and sprinkle with a bit of sugar to prevent a skin. Let cool.
Note: Serve mixed or topped with whipped cream.

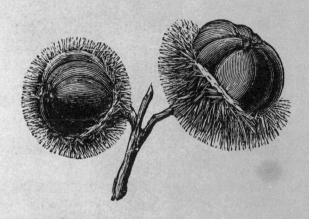

## Vermicelles
## (Chestnut Purée)

Chestnuts are still very plentiful in the southern part of Switzerland, the Ticino region. Vermicelles, a popular dessert throughout Switzerland, originated here. The name stems from "vermicelli", which are long, thin noodles.

*800 g (1½ lbs) chestnuts, salt, 1½-2 dl (½-¾ C) milk,*
*1 vanilla bean, 80 g (¼ C 3 Tbs) sugar, 5 Tbs cream,*
*2 Tbs cherry schnaps, 2 dl (¾ C) cream*

Using a sharp pointed knife, slash the chestnuts on their rounded side. Roast in the oven or on a grill until the shells pop open. Or, you may also boil them in lightly salted water for 5 minutes. Remove the tough outer shell and the brown inner skin with a knife. Place the nuts in a saucepan, cover with lightly salted water. Cover the pan and cook for 40-50 minutes. When the chestnuts are tender, put them through a purée strainer. Bring the milk and slit vanilla bean to a boil. Add the puréed chestnuts. Stir until it forms a thick paste. Remove the vanilla bean, pour in the cherry schnaps and cool.

Before serving, pass through a sieve (medium-sized holes), chestnuts press or meat grinder directly onto the serving dishes. Garnish with whipped cream.

Note: You may enhance this delicacy by garnishing it with pieces of meringue. Serve either in small dessert bowls or on a large platter.

121

# Meringues

In the Emmen valley and the Bern highlands meringues are usually served after a festive meal. The name is said to come from the city of Meiringen; and because foreign guests could not pronounce the original name "Meiringerli", in time it evolved into "Meringues".

### For approx. 10 portions

*4 egg whites from fresh eggs, 200 g (1 C) sugar, butter, flour, 4 dl (1½ C) cream, 1 Tbs sugar*

Beat the egg whites until foamy. Gradually add half of the sugar in spoonfuls, continuing to beat. When the mixture is stiff, carefully fold in all but a tsp of the remaining sugar. Using a spoon or pastry bag, shape the meringue paste into oblong mounds onto a greased baking sheet lightly dusted with flour. Set them a few centimeters apart. Dust the meringues lightly with sugar and let dry in a very low oven for 1 hour. Keep the oven door ajar. They may take on just a bit of color and should be firm on the outside and dry on the inside. Let them dry out for a few more minutes after turning off the oven. Remove from the sheet with a spatula and let cool. Keep the meringues in a tin box.

Before serving, whip the cream with 1 Tbs sugar. Fill it into two meringues per serving.

*Heavenly . . .*

# Wine Toast

*3 Tbs raisins, 3 dl (1¼ C) red wine, 3 Tbs sugar, 1 cinnamon stick, 1 tsp grated lemon rind, 4-8 thin slices white bread (French or Italian), 2 Tbs butter*

Wash and drain the raisins, then place in a skillet with the red wine. Let stand for 15 minutes. Add the sugar, broken up cinnamon stick and lemon rind and simmer over high heat. Brown the bread on both sides in butter. Pour the wine sauce over the bread and serve.

# Notes and more recipes

Fig. 12

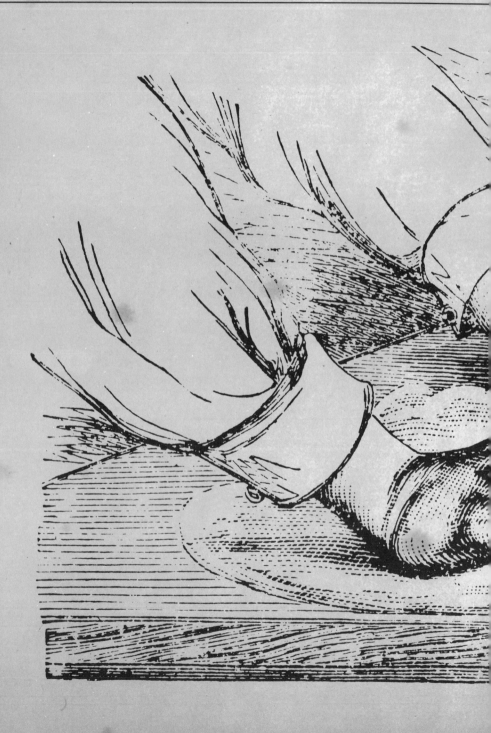

# Cakes and Pies, Cookies

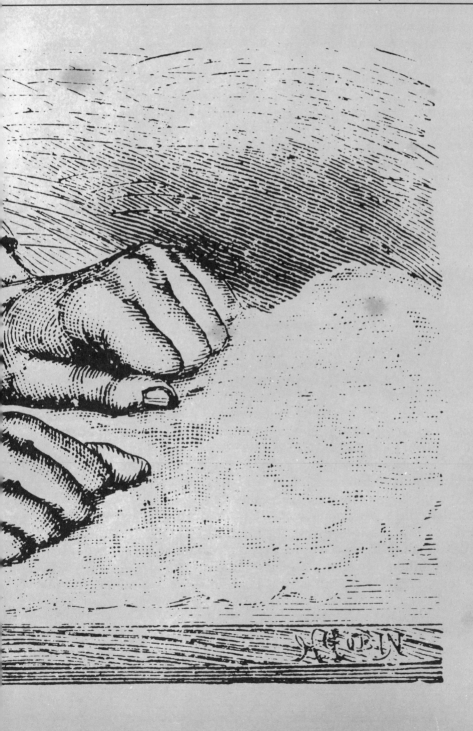

## a) Cakes and Pies

The bakers of the Engadine region have been famous for centuries. When times became hard many of them left their home towns and immigrated to America and Australia. The more successful ones eventually returned and shared their experience, leading to the creation of many original cakes and pies. The most famous is probably the Engadine nut pie, which can be relatively easily made at home. Other popular specialities include the "Bündner Schokoladentorte", a chocolate cake made from ground bread and chocolate, the Aargau carrot cake and the St. Gallen monastery pie which owes its recipe to the monastery of St. Gallen.

Switzerland's fruit pies reflect the current season.

The Thurgau apple pie and the Valaisian apricot pie are especially delicious.

### Engadine Nut Cake

*300 g (2½ C) flour, 200 g (7 oz) butter, 1 pinch salt, 400 g (2 C) sugar, 2 eggs, 125 g (4 oz) walnut kernels, 125 g (4 oz) hazelnuts or almonds, 2½ dl (1 C) cream, butter for the pan*

Mix the flour, butter (cut into pieces), 150 g (¾ C) sugar, salt and beaten eggs into a dough. Do not knead, or else it will become stiff. Set in a cool place for at least 30 minutes.

Melt the remaining sugar in a dry pan without stirring until caramelized and light brown in color. Add the nuts. After a few minutes pour in the cream and let thicken slightly.

Roll the dough and line a greased spring-form (removable – rim pan) with ⅔ of it. Spread with the nut mixture. Fold back the edges of the dough. Make a top crust with the remaining dough and place over the filling. Moisten the edges and pinch them together. Prick the top several times with a fork. Place in a cold oven and bake at

180° C (356° F) for 60-70 minutes. Be careful that the crust does not get too dark. If necessary, protect it with a sheet of aluminum foil. Note: You may enhance the cake by mixing 1 Tbs honey into the nut mixture while it is still in the pan. Then spread the dough with red-currant jelly before adding the nut filling.

## Bündner Chocolate Cake

*6 egg yolks, 200 g (1 C) sugar, 150 g (5 oz) unpeeled ground almonds, 100 g (3¹/₂ oz) day-old grated brown bread, 80 g (2³/₄ oz) butter, 200 g (7 oz) semi-sweet chocolate, 6 egg whites, 1 pinch salt, butter for the pan, 1 Tbs toasted bread crumbs*

Beat the egg yolk with the sugar until creamy. Stir in the almonds, bread and melted butter. Melt the chocolate in 2 tablespoons water over low heat in a small saucepan and add to the dough.
Beat the egg whites with a dash salt until stiff and carefully fold into the dough. Grease a spring-form pan with butter and sprinkle with bread crumbs. Pour in the dough and bake for 50-60 minutes in a preheated 180° C (356° F) oven.

## Rahmfladen
## (Sour Cream Cake)

*¹/₂ L (2 C) sour cream, 100 g (³/₄ C) flour, salt, pepper, anise, coriander, 500 g (18 oz) Pâte Brisée (see page 108), butter for the pan, 50 g (¹/₄ C) honey or molasses*

Add the flour and spices to the sour cream and stir into a smooth dough. It should be somewhat thicker than pancake batter. Grease a baking sheet and line it with the rolled Pâte Brisée. Spread with the sour cream mixture and bake in a preheated 180° C (356° F) oven for 30-40 minutes. Serve lukewarm spread with honey or molasses, and white coffee.
Note: This is a very old recipe. In more recent versions, 1-2 beaten eggs are substituted for a portion of the flour and mixed with the sour cream instead.

# Rüeblitorte
## (Carrot Cake)

*For a 24 cm (9 in) spring-form: 5 egg yolks, 1 Tbs grated lemon rind, 300 g (1½ C) sugar, 300 g (10½ oz) carrots, 300 g (10½ oz) ground almonds, 4 Tbs flour or cornstarch, ½ tsp cinnamon, 1 pinch ground cloves, 1 tsp baking-powder, 1 pinch salt, 2 Tbs kirsch or rum (as desired), 5 egg whites, 3 Tbs apricot marmalade*
*For the glaze: 150 g (1½ C) confectioners' sugar, ½ egg white, 2 Tbs lemon juice or kirsch*

Beat the egg yolks, lemon rind and sugar until creamy. Peel and grate the carrots. Immediately fold in the eggs together with the almonds. Add the flour or cornstarch, cinnamon, cloves, baking-powder and salt. Pour in the kirsch or rum. Fold in the stiff egg whites. Fill the dough into the spring-form. Bake for 60 minutes at 190° C (375° F).
Spread the lukewarm surface with apricot marmalade. Mix the ingredients for the glaze and pour over the cake. Spread the glaze in a circular motion over the top and sides of the cake. (You may also forgo the glaze and simply sprinkle the cooled cake with confectioners' sugar.)

## Monastery Pie

*For a round 24 cm (9 in) pie pan: 300 g (2½ C) flour, 1 tsp baking-powder, 120 g (½ C 2 Tbs) sugar, 125 g (4 oz) ground almonds, 150 g (5 oz) butter, 1½ tsp cinnamon, 1 Tbs sweetened chocolate-powder, 1 pinch ground cloves, 2-3 Tbs milk, some butter and flour for the pan, 1 jar thick red-currant or raspberry marmalade, 1 egg yolk*

Sift the flour and baking-powder into a bowl. Add the sugar and almonds, followed by flakes of butter. Work the mixture into a crumbly mass with your fingers. Add the cinnamon, chocolate, cloves and milk and quickly mix into a dough. Cover or wrap the dough in a damp cloth and chill in the refrigerator for a few hours.
Grease the pan with butter and dust with flour. Line with ⅔ of the rolled dough. Roll out the remaining dough and cut into strips with a biscuit cutter. Place one strip around the bottom edges. Add and

evenly spread the marmalade. Use remaining dough strips to make a lattice. Brush the edges and lattice with beaten egg yolk. Bake the pie in a 180° C (356° F) preheated oven for 45 minutes.

Note: This pie may be kept for a few days and is thus ideal to prepare in advance.

## Apricot Pie

*For a 24 cm (9 in) pie pan: 125 g (1 C) flour, 25 g (2 Tbs) pork fat, 50 g (4 Tbs) butter, 1 pinch salt, 2 Tbs sugar, 1 egg, 500 g (18 oz) apricots, 1 Tbs sugar, 1/2 tsp flour, 1 dash cinnamon*

Sift flour into a bowl. Cut the butter and fat into flakes. Add salt and sugar. Using your fingers, mix all ingredients until a crumbly mixture forms. Lightly beat the egg and add to the flour mixture. Quickly work into a dough. Add 1-2 Tbs water as needed. Form the dough into a ball and let rest for at least 1 hour. Halve and pit the apricots. Roll out the dough 3 mm (1/10 in) thick. Combine the remaining sugar, flour and cinnamon and sprinkle over the dough. Cover densely with the halved or quartered apricots. Bake at 200° C (390° F) for 35-40 minutes. After 15 minutes sprinkle with sugar as desired. Serve lukewarm or cold, but always fresh.

129

# Almond and Prune Pie

*500 g (18 oz) Pâte Brisée (see page 108), confec-*
*tioners' sugar*
*For the almond filling: 30 g (2 Tbs) butter, 5 Tbs*
*sugar, 2 Tbs honey, 1 egg, 150 g (5 oz) peeled ground*
*almonds, 1 Tbs cream, 1 Tbs rosewater, juice and*
*rind of 1 lemon*
*For the prune filling: 300 g (10½ oz) pitted dried*
*prunes, 1 pinch cinnamon, 1 Tbs sugar, 1 Tbs kirsch*

First prepare the 2 fillings:
For the almond filling, beat the butter with the sugar until creamy.
Add and combine with the honey, almonds, beaten egg, cream, rosewater and lemon juice and rind.
Place the prunes in a bowl and cover with boiling water. Let stand
for 2 hours, then drain thoroughly. Put the prunes through a ricer
and mix with suger, cinnamon and kirsch. If necessary, add some of
the liquid from the prunes to give you a firm jam.
Roll the dough out 3 mm (¹/₁₀ in) thick into a large rectangle. Cut out
2 rounds, making one 2 cm (¾ in) larger than the other. Place the
larger one in a round, rinsed cake pan (9 in). Spread one half with
the almond paste and the other half with the prune jam, leaving a
2 cm (¾ in) edge all the way around. Slit the smaller round with a
sharp pointed knife parallel to the edge 8-10 times. These slits will
open into almond shaped ovals allowing the dark and light colored
fillings to show through when the pie is done. After slitting the
cover, carefully place it over the filling. Moisten the edges with water
and seal firmly with a fork. Bake for 15-20 minutes in a preheated
230° C (450° F) oven, then reduce the heat to 200° C (390° F). Bake
for about 30 minutes longer. Let cool on a grate. Sprinkle with confectioners' sugar before serving.

## Fruit Juice Pie

*For a round 24 cm (9 in) pie pan: 300 g (10½ oz)*
*Pâte Brisée (see page 108), butter for the pan, 1 tsp*
*cornstarch, 1 Tbs sugar, 2 Tbs milk, 2 Tbs cream,*
*1 egg, 2 dl (¾ C) concentrated fruit juice, 30 g*
*(1 Tbs) butter flakes*

Roll out dough to 3 mm (¹/₁₀ in) thickness. Grease the pie pan and line with the dough. Prick several times with a fork. In a bowl, combine cornstarch, sugar, milk, cream, egg and fruit juice concentrate. Spread on the dough and dot with butter. Bake for 30 minutes in a preheated 220° C (428° F) oven. Check often to prevent bubbles from forming on the surface and so that the crust does not get too dark. If necessary, cover with a sheet of aluminum foil.

## Tarte au Vin Vaudois
## (Vaudois Wine Cake)

*For a 24 cm (9 in) pie pan: 300 g (10½ oz) Pâte Brisée (see page 108), butter for the pan, 2 Tbs flour, 80 g (⅓ C 1 Tbs) sugar, 2 dl (¾ C) white or red wine, butter flakes, ½ tsp cinnamon*

Roll the dough out to a thickness of 3 mm (¹⁄₁₀ in) and place in a greased, round pie pan. Prick several times with a fork. Sprinkle the flour and half of the sugar evenly onto the dough. Carefully pour over the wine. Dot with butter and sprinkle with the cinnamon and remaining sugar. Bake for 30 minutes in a preheated 240° C (465°F) oven.
Note: Before being poured onto the dough, the wine is often mixed with a few tablespoons of cream.

## Thurgau Apple Pie

*80 g (2¾ oz) butter, 1 pinch salt, 3⅓ Tbs sugar, 3 eggs, 1 Tbs cream, 125 g (1 C 1 Tbs) flour, 250 g (9 oz) chopped almonds, 5 apples, butter for the pan, 4 Tbs raspberry marmalade*

Whip the butter until foamy. Stir in 1½ Tbs sugar, 1 beaten egg and the cream. Gradually fold in the sifted flour. Let rest in a cool place for 1 hour. For the filling, whip the remaining eggs and 2 Tbs sugar until creamy. Add the almonds, then grate in two unpared, washed apples. Pare, core and halve the remaining apples. Roll out the dough and place it in a greased 9 inch pie pan. Spread with the almond mixture. Place the apples halves on a wooden board, flat side down. Thinly slice the apple halves; but not all the way through so that the slices are still connected. Arrange the apples in the pie

131

shell. Bake for 40 minutes at 230° C (450° F). In the last 5 minutes of baking, spread the apples with 2 tablespoons marmalade. Remove from oven and spread with the remaining marmalade.

## b) Cookies

In the German part of Switzerland, Christmas without Christmas cookies is something unimaginable. By the end of November or at the latest during Advent nearly all households are busy kneading dough and making all shapes and sizes of cookies to be kept in tin boxes until Christmas. The children are eager helpers especially when it comes to decorating the cookies with different glazes and sugar.

Every family usually has recipes that were handed down from generation to generation including such traditional favorites as "Mailänderli", "Cinnamon Stars", "Leckerli", "Chräbeli" and "Brunsli", all described in the following chapter.

## Amaretti
## (Almond Cookies)

A Ticino almond pastry which tastes delicious with coffee.

> *270 g (1 C) sweet almonds, 30 g (1 oz) bitter almonds,*
> *300 g (1½ C) sugar, 2-3 egg whites, confectioners'*
> *sugar, 1 Tbs flour*

Blanche the almonds. Pinch or rub off the skins. Spread on a cookie sheet and dry in a low oven for 1 hour. When the almonds are dry, grind them finely in a nut grinder. Add sugar. Grind both together until you have an even mixture. Lightly beat the egg whites and gradually add to the almonds. Mix into a firm batter.

Place in small balls on a floured cookie sheet. Squeeze them slightly on both sides using your thumb and forefinger. This gives them their well known shape. Let stand overnight. On the following day, sprinkle with confectioners' sugar and bake in a 180° C (356° F) oven.

# Chräbeli
## (Anise Crescents)

*3 eggs, 300 g (1½ C) sugar, 1 Tbs kirsch, 1 dash salt,*
*1 heaping tsp anise, 400 g (1⅓ C) flour, butter for the*
*pan*

Beat the eggs and sugar with an electric mixer for 10 minutes until creamy, add the anise, kirsch and salt. Stir in the sifted flour; the exact quantity of flour depends on the size of the eggs. The dough should be firm enough to easily form into a ball. Let cool overnight. On the following day, shape the dough into 1½ cm (½ in) thick cylinders. Then cut them into 5 cm (2 in) long pieces and make 3 diagonal slits at equal distance apart to the middle of the pieces. Bend slightly to form crescents and place them on a greased baking sheet. Let dry at room temperature for 24 hours. Bake at 160° C (320° F) for about 15 minutes. Be careful that the "Chräbeli" do not take on any color. The underside should remain light as well.
Note: After baking, these pastries are hard. They will become soft if left in the open for 3-4 days. Then place them in a tin box for 2-3 weeks. After that they are ready to be eaten.

# Mailänderli
## (Sweet Cookies)

*4 eggs, 250 g (1¼ C) sugar, 250 g (9 oz) butter, 1 pinch*
*salt, 500 g (1 lb) flour, ½ Tbs grated lemon rind, 2 egg*
*yolks*

Beat eggs and sugar into a white cream. Fold in the lukewarm, melted butter, salt and sifted flour. Add lemon rind. Let stand for 1 hour or even better cool overnight. Roll out 3 mm (¹/₁₀ in) thick. Using a cookie cutter, form into any shape you wish and place on a greased cookie sheet. Brush twice with the beaten egg yolks. Bake in a 160° C (320° F) preheated oven for about 20 minutes.

133

# Basle Leckerli
## (Honey Pastries)

*500 g (1¹/₃ C) firm honey, 350 g (1³/₄ C) sugar, 2 Tbs cinnamon, 1 pinch ground cloves, 1 tsp ground nutmeg, 125 g (4 oz) almonds, 125 g (4 oz) hazelnuts, 100 g (3¹/₂ oz) each candied orange and lemon peel, rind of 1 lemon, 700 g (5³/₄ C) flour, 2 pinches washed potash, 2 dl (³/₄ C) kirsch*
*For the glaze: 150 g (³/₄ C) sugar, 1 dl (¹/₃ C) water*

Bring to a boil, honey, sugar, cinnamon, nutmeg and cloves. Chop the almonds and hazelnuts. Coarsely chop the candied orange and lemon peel together with the lemon rind. Add with the nuts to the honey mixture. Remove the pan from the heat. Gradually sift in ⅔ of the flour and the potash. Add the kirsch. Place the remaining flour on a wooden board. Pour over the dough and quickly knead together. Divide the dough in half. Roll out both halves and place them on two rectangular, floured baking sheets. Let rest overnight. Bake for 15-20 minutes in a preheated 230° C (450° F) oven. Remove from oven and immediately cut out small rectangles with a pointed knife, but only ¾ of the way through the dough. To prepare the glaze, bring the sugar and water to a boil, then simmer for another 5 minutes until the syrup is stringy. Remove the pieces from the baking sheet, brush off excess flour and spread with the hot glaze. Now cut the pieces all the way through and let dry.

# Basle Brunsli
## (Almond Chocolate Cookies)

*450 g (1 lb) unpeeled ground almonds, 400 g (4¹/₂ C) confectioners' sugar, 75 g (3 oz) unsweetened chocolate-powder, 3 egg whites, 2 Tbs kirsch, 1 pinch each cinnamon and nutmeg powder, 100 g (¹/₂ C) coarse sugar*

Mix all ingredients with the lightly whipped egg whites. If the dough is too moist, add more almonds. Dust your table or wooden board with the coarse sugar and roll the dough 1 cm (⅓ in) thick on it. Sprinkle the dough with sugar as well, then cut out hearts, crosses and clover leaves with a cookie cutter. Place the cookies 2 cm (¾ in) apart on a well greased baking sheet. Let dry at room temperature for 1 hour. Do not refrigerate.

Slide the baking sheet onto the top rack of the oven. Bake for 5 minutes at 180° C (356° F). The surface of the cookies should develop a light crust but not change color. Leave on the sheet 2-3 minutes after baking. Remove with a spatula and place on a cooling rack. Put the still slightly warm cookies in a tin (or plastic bag for freezing). They will dry out at once if left out in the open.

## Cinnamon Stars

*2 egg whites, 250 g (1¼ C) sugar, 1 Tbs cinnamon,*
*250 g (9 oz) ground unblanched almonds, 1 Tbs*
*lemon juice, 1 tsp grated lemon rind, sugar, 120-150 g*
*(1½ C) confectioners' sugar*

Whip egg whites until stiff. Add sugar and cinnamon and whip for another 10 minutes. Set aside 5 Tbs of the mixture for the glaze. Fold the almonds and lemon juice into the remainder and knead into a dough. Let stand for 15 minutes. Dust a board or table densely with confectioners' sugar. Roll out the dough to a thickness of ⅓ inch. Cut with a star cutter. Line a cookie sheet with wax paper and place the cookies on it. Let rest for 30 minutes. For the glaze, mix the reserved egg mixture with confectioners' sugar until it thickens. Carefully brush the tops of the cookies with the glaze. Bake in a preheated 200° C (390° F) oven for about 15 minutes.

## Totebeinli
## (Hazelnut "Legs")

This candy is mostly found in the region around Graubünden.

*250 g (9 oz) hazelnuts, 50 g (4 Tbs) butter, 250 g*
*(1¼ C) sugar, 250 g (2 C) flour, 2 eggs, juice of*
*1 orange, grated rind of ½ lemon, 1 Tbs cinnamon*

Chop the nuts coarsely. Beat the butter until foamy. Combine all ingredients. Form the dough into finger-sized rolls of any desired length. Place on a baking sheet and bake in a preheated 160° C (320° F) oven for 15 minutes.

135

## Hazelnut Delights

*240 g (8½ oz) ground hazelnuts, 240 g (8½ oz) un-
peeled ground almonds, 480 g (2⅓ C) sugar, 3 Tbs
finely chopped candied orange and lemon rind, 1 Tbs
lemon juice, 1 Tbs cinnamon, 1 pinch star anise,
2 Tbs honey, 40 g (3 Tbs) flour, 4 egg whites, 65 g
(⅓ C) confectioners' sugar, 1 Tbs butter
For the glaze: 65 g (⅓ C) confectioners' sugar, 2 Tbs
plum schnaps*

Roast the hazelnuts in a dry skillet over medium heat, stirring constantly. Let cool. Place in a bowl and mix with the almonds, sugar,
candied orange and lemon rind, honey and spices. Fold in the stiff
egg whites. Using your hands, work the mixture into a smooth dough
which can be easily kneaded. Let rest for 1 hour.

Dust a board with confectioners' sugar and roll out the dough on it
to a thickness of 6 mm (¼ in). Cut out small rectangles (if you use a
wooden mold, repeatedly rinse then dip it in confectioners' sugar).
Place the cookies on a greased baking sheet and let dry for 3-4 hours.
Slide in the top rung of the oven and dry for 5-7 minutes at 200° C
(390° F). Larger ones take 2-3 minutes longer. Mix the sifted confectioners' sugar and plum schnaps and brush the glaze over the
warm pastries.

# Notes and more recipes

fig ·13 **Traditional Holiday a**

# Deep-Fried Pastries, Sundries

## a) Traditional Holiday Pastries

Switzerland has many pastries and sweets that were traditionally only prepared on certain holidays, and still today they are considered as something special.

The most well known recipes are included in this chapter.

## Bern Braid

In Bern, no holiday, wedding or baptism is complete without a Bern Braid. Over the years it has also evolved into the "Sunday bread", and since they are not open on Sundays the bakeries are sold out by Saturday afternoon.

On St. Nicolas day many bakeries sell the Braid in the shape of a little man called "Grittibänz".

*1 kg (2.2 lbs) bleached, all-purpose flour, 30 g (1 oz)*
*fresh yeast, 1 tsp sugar, ½ L (2 C) lukewarm milk,*
*160-200 g (5½-7 oz) fresh butter, 2 tsp salt, 2 eggs,*
*1 egg yolk, butter for the pan*
*To spread: 2 egg yolks, 1 pinch salt*

Sift the flour into a large slightly warmed bowl. Make a well in the center and fill it with finely crumbled yeast. Sprinkle with sugar, then pour over 1 cup lukewarm (max. 35° C / 95° F) milk. Stir with two fingers until the yeast is dissolved. Add a bit of flour and mix into a leaven. Cover the bowl and keep warm (in the oven at max. 35° C / 95° F).

Cover the risen leaven with flour. Sprinkle the flour with salt, dot with the butter and add the beaten eggs. Slowly pour in the remaining lukewarm milk and work into a firm dough. Knead the dough until it is smooth and comes away from the sides of the bowl. Cover and let rise again in a warm place for 1½ hours.

Divide the dough into two equal parts. Shape both into long, tapered rolls. Place one roll crosswise over the middle of the other. Grab the two ends of the horizontal roll. Take the left end and place it to the right and the right end and place it to the left over the vertical roll.

Now take the ends of the vertical roll and repeat the above procedure, thus making a braid. Finish by tucking the ends under. Place the braid on a slightly greased baking sheet and let rise for 10 minutes in a warm place. Brush with egg yolk beaten with salt and cool for 30 minutes. Place in a cold oven and bake at 240° C (465° F) for 40-50 minutes.

## Fruit Bread

*750 g (1½ lbs) yeast dough (see page 140), 350 g (12 oz) dried pears, 150 g (5 oz) dried pitted prunes, 100 g (3½ oz) raisins, 1 Tbs kirsch or plum liqueur, 100 g (3½ oz) walnuts, 50 g (¼ C) sugar, 1 tsp cinnamon, 1 pinch ground cloves, 1 egg yolk*

Soak the prunes and pears overnight in cold water. Simmer the next day in the same liquid for 20 minutes. Drain and put through a meat grinder or ricer. Soak the raisins in the liqueur for 30 minutes. Then add to the fruit together with the chopped nuts, sugar and spices. Knead ⅓ of the dough with the fruit mixture and shape 2 loaves. Roll the remaining dough into a square. Cut the square in half and wrap one half around each loaf. Moisten the edges with water and press them together. Place the loaves with the seam side down onto a large baking sheet. Prick the surface several times with a fork. Let rise in a warm place (35° C / 95° F). Brush with the beaten egg yolk and bake in a preheated 170° C (338° F) oven for 1 hour.

## Cuquettes
## (Flatbreads)

*1 egg yolk, 2 Tbs sugar, 3 dl (1½ C) double cream, 1 pinch salt, 400 g (3⅓ C) flour, 100 g (3½ oz) butter, sugar*

Beat the egg yolk with the sugar until creamy. Stir in the cream and salt. Gradually add the sifted flour and work into a firm dough. Let cool for 1 hour. Roll the dough into a 1 cm (⅓ in) thick rectangle. Dot evenly with butter. Fold the dough 4 times. Let cool for 10 min-

141

utes. Roll again 2-3 times and refold as above. Let rest in a cool place for 12-24 hours.

Cut out small rounds and roll them out very thin (2 mm / $^1/_{10}$ in) until they are the size of a dessert plate. Using a cookie cutter, make 1$^1/_2$ cm ($^1/_2$ in) parallel slits, leaving an edge of 2 cm ($^3/_4$ in) all the way around, so that they don't fall apart. Place the flatbreads on a greased baking sheet, sprinkle with sugar and bake for 15-20 minutes in a preheated 220° C (428° F) oven until lightly browned. Let cool completely before stacking.

## Fruit Roll

On St. Nicolas day, the 6th of December, it is customary in nearly all of Switzerland to bake Lebkuchen and fruit breads. Those who do not wish to bake themselves can, of course, buy them in any bakery. St. Nicolas day without Lebkuchen and fruitbread would be a big disappointment, especially for the children.

> *For the dough: 300 g (2$^1/_2$ C) flour, 150 g (5 oz) butter, 2 eggs, 1 pinch salt (or: 500 g / 18 oz Pâte Brisée, see page 108)*
> *For the filling: 1 kg (2.2 lbs) dried pears, 300 g (10$^1/_2$ oz) dried prunes, 100 g (3$^1/_2$ oz) figs, 200 g (7 oz) chopped walnuts, 100 g (3$^1/_2$ oz) raisins, 150 g ($^3/_4$ C) sugar, 1 Tbs cinnamon, $^1/_2$ tsp star anise, 2 pinches ground cloves, 1 dl ($^1/_3$ C) kirsch, 1 egg*

Sift the flour into a bowl and make a well in the middle. Fill with the beaten eggs, salt and soft butter (room temperature). Quickly work into a dough. Form a ball and let stand for 1 hour.

Soak the dried prunes in cold water for at least 12 hours. Then simmer in the same liquid for 30 minutes. Drain, remove stems and stone and chop on a wooden board with the nuts. Add the raisins, sugar, spices and kirsch and mix into a smooth mixture.

Roll the dough into a rectangular shape. Spread it with the filling, leaving a 2 cm ($^3/_4$ in) edge on all sides. Fold the edges over the filling, then roll up the dough and shape into a flat rectangle. Brush the ends with egg white and pinch them together. Brush the cake with egg yolk and prick several times with a fork. Place on a baking sheet and bake in a preheated 180° C (356° F) oven for 30-40 minutes.

# Lebkuchen

*For a round 26 cm (10 in) cake pan: 2½ dl (1 C) sour cream, 2 dl (¾ C) honey, ½ dl (2 Tbs) kirsch, 100 g (½ C) sugar, 40 g (3 Tbs) candied orange and lemon peel, ½ tsp cinnamon, ½ tsp anise, 1 pinch each ground nutmeg and cloves, 1 pinch salt, 1 tsp double-acting baking-powder, 500 g (1 lb) all-purpose flour, 1½ dl (½ C) milk, 2 Tbs honey to brush the cake*

Combine the cream, honey, kirsch, sugar and spices. Sift the flour and baking-powder and add to honey and cream mixture. Add the milk and work into a smooth dough. Pat the dough into the pan and bake in a preheated 180° C (356° F) oven for 40-45 minutes. Brush with honey while still warm.

Serve the Lebkuchen with fresh butter, honey or sweetened whipped cream.

## Schwyz Fruit Cake

*For the dough: 250 g (2 C 1 Tbs) flour, 1 pinch salt, 2 Tbs sugar, 120 g (4 oz) butter, 1 egg, 2-3 Tbs cream, 1 tsp grated lemon rind, butter*
*For the filling: 250 g (9 oz) dried pears, 250 g (9 oz) pitted prunes, 100 g (3½ oz) chopped nuts, 1 pinch each cinnamon and clove-powder, 1 Tbs lemon juice, 2-3 Tbs sugar*
*For the glaze: 2 dl (¾ C) cream, 3 Tbs fruit concentrate*

Soak the pears and prunes in cold water for 1-2 days.

For the dough, work the flour, salt, sugar and butter with your fingers into a crumbly mixture. Beat the egg, mix it with the cream and lemon rind and add to the flour mixture. Quickly work into a smooth dough. Form into a ball and let stand for 1 hour. Drain the fruit well. Remove the stems from the pears. Put the fruit through a ricer or finely chop it by hand. Combine with nuts, spices, lemon juice and sugar. Place the dough onto a greased baking sheet. Spread evenly with the fruit mixture. Combine the cream with the fruit concentrate and pour over the cake. Bake in a 220° C (428° F) preheated oven for 30-35 minutes.

143

# Easter Cake

The cake can be prepared with a semolina, rice or bakers' cheese-filling. This is an old recipe from Lucerne.

*For the dough: 250 g flour, 125 g butter, 1 pinch salt, 2 dl water*
*For the filling: 5 dl (2 C) milk, $^{1}/_{4}$ tsp salt, 125 g (4 oz) rice, 125 g ($^{1}/_{2}$ C 2 Tbs) sugar, 3 egg yolks, 1 tsp grated lemon rind, 1 dl ($^{1}/_{3}$ C) cream, 120 g (4 oz) peeled ground almonds, 3 Tbs raisins, 3 egg whites, butter for the pan*

Combine the flour and flakes of butter with your fingers. Dissolve the salt in 2 dl ($^{3}/_{4}$ C) water. Add to the flour and quickly work into a dough. Do not knead. Let stand for 1 hour.
Bring to a boil the milk, salt and 1 dl ($^{1}/_{3}$ C) water. Add the rice. Simmer for 40-50 minutes over low heat until thick. Stir occasionally, carefully. Beat the sugar with the egg yolks until creamy. Add the lemon rind, cream, almonds and raisins and stir into the cooled rice porridge. Fold in the stiff egg whites. Grease a medium-sized spring-form (removable − rim pan) with butter. Line the pan with the dough, making a 4 cm (1½ in) high edge. Spread with filling and bake for 1 hour at 200° C (390° F).

## Torta di Pane
## (Bread Cake)

A bread cake made on church holidays in the Ticino.

*300 g (10½ oz) stale bread, $^{3}/_{4}$ L (3 C) milk, 1 vanilla bean, 3 eggs, 160 g ($^{3}/_{4}$ C) sugar, 1 pinch salt, 1 tsp grated lemon rind, 100 g (3½ oz) chopped, candied fruit, 1 tsp cinnamon, 1 Tbs grappa (grapeliqueur), 2 Tbs butter, 2 Tbs almond slivers*

Cut the bread into small pieces and place into a bowl. Scald the milk together with the vanilla bean and pour over the bread. Let stand for 1-2 hours, then put through a strainer. Beat eggs, sugar and salt until foamy. Add, along with candied fruit, cinnamon and grappa to the bread mixture. Combine ingredients into a smooth dough. Generously grease a round cake pan, then sprinkle with bread crumbs and pour in the dough. Sprinkle with almond slivers. Bake in a 180° C

144

(356° F) preheated oven for 60-70 minutes. Remove immediately from pan and cool. This cake is good for several days.

Note: For this particular recipe it is worthwhile to line the pan with baking foil. Then it is not necessary to grease and coat the pan with flour.

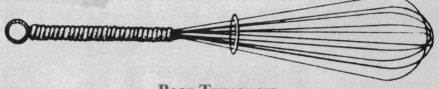

## Pear Turnovers

This is a very tasty pastry from Geneva; it is made with preserved pears and various spices.

*For the dough: 250 g (2 C) flour, 60 g (¹/₄ C) pork fat, 60 g (2 oz) butter, 1 dl (¹/₃ C) water, 1 egg yolk, ¹/₄ tsp salt*
*For the filling: 1 kg (2.2 lbs) ripe pears, sugar (depending on the weight of the cooked pears), 100 g (3¹/₂ oz) finely chopped candied orange and lemon peel, 2 Tbs raisins, 1 tsp cinnamon, 3 Tbs white wine*

Quarter and core the unpeeled pears. Place in a saucepan and cover with water. Simmer over low heat until very tender. Pour the pears into a sieve lined with a cheesecloth. Drain well, then rub through a ricer. Weigh the pear puree and return to the pan with an equal amount of sugar. Stirring constantly, cook the pears into a dark jam. Be careful that it does not stick to the pan. Add the candied lemon and orange peel, wine, raisins and cinnamon and cook for another 5 minutes.

Mix the flour, salt, pork fat and butter with your fingers. Add the water and quickly work into a smooth dough. Let rest for 1 hour. Roll the dough to a thickness of 3 mm (¹/₁₀ in). Cut out 10 cm (4 in) rounds. Mix a portion of the jam with the remaining wine. Place a tsp of filling onto each round. Moisten the edges with water, fold over and seal firmly with a fork. Prick and bake in a preheated 200° C (390° F) oven for 20 minutes. Serve lukewarm or cold.

Note: The rest of the jam may be reheated, filled into jars or an earthenware pot and sealed immediately. The preserves may be kept this way for several months.

## b) Deep-Fried Pastries

On the occasion of the carnival or church holidays it is traditional to serve various deep-fried pastries. The basic ingredients, flour, eggs, milk or cream are pretty much the same everywhere. What comes out in the end, however, may be very different from one region to another. This chapter offers a cross-section of these deliciously fragrant specialities, which can be bought in almost any pastry shop.

## Apple Fritters

*6 larges apples, fat for frying, 1 Tbs sugar, 1 tsp cinnamon*
*For the fritter batter: 150 g (1¼ C) flour, 1 dl (⅓ C) milk, 1 tsp oil, 1 pinch salt, 2 eggs*

Combine the flour, milk, 1 dl (⅓ C) water, salt and oil. Separate the eggs and add the yolks. Beat this mixture until smooth. Rest for 1 hour.
Peel and core the apples. Cut crosswise, about 1 cm (⅓ in) thick. Dip into the batter and fry in batches in the hot fat until light brown. Drain on a paper towel and dust with cinnamon sugar. Serve immediately.
Note: They taste delicious served with vanilla sauce.
The same batter may be used to make sage leaf fritters which serve as an original garnishment for meat and fish dishes. Dip the whole sage leaves in the batter, holding them by their stems. Fry them in the deep fat for 1-2 minutes. You may also serve them with an aperitif, a glass of wine or, sprinkled with cinnamon sugar, with coffee.

146

# Nidwaldner Chilbikrapfen
## (Turnovers)

*½ L (2 C) milk, 150 g (5 oz) butter, 1 tsp salt, 1 kg (2.2 lbs) flour, fat for deep-frying, cinnamon sugar made from 4 Tbs sugar and 1 tsp cinnamon*
*For the filling: 1 kg (2.2 lbs) bakers' cheese, finely grated rind of 1 lemon, 50 g (2 oz) raisins, 8 Tbs sugar, 1 tsp cinnamon*

Bring the milk to a boil. Slice the butter and add to the milk. Cool slightly. Gradually add the salt and flour and work into a firm dough. Place the bakers' cheese into a bowl. Knead, press and drain the cheese; then add the lemon rind, washed raisins, sugar and cinnamon. Roll out the dough 3 mm (⅒ in) thick. Cut it into rhombuses with a cutter. Place a teaspoon of filling onto each diamond. Bring the moistened edges together and pinch to form a triangle. Drop into the fat and fry until golden brown. Sprinkle or coat with cinnamon sugar.

*This really tastes great!*

## Strübli

*3 dl (1¼ C) milk, 1 pinch salt, 2 Tbs butter, 250 g (2 C) flour, 2 Tbs white wine, 3 eggs, fat for deep-frying, cinnamon sugar from 4 Tbs sugar and 1 tsp cinnamon*

Bring the milk and salt to a boil. Add the butter and let it melt. Sift the flour onto a paper towel or plate. Stir into the milk, all at one time. Beat in the egg yolks one by one. Whip the egg whites until they are stiff. Pour the batter over the stiff egg whites and carefully mix together. Add the wine. The batter should be fluid enough to pour it through a funnel. Add more liquid if necessary (wine or milk). Ladle batches of batter through a funnel into the hot fat. Move the funnel in a circular motion so that the batter forms into swirls. Fry the "Strübli" until delicately browned. Drain and serve warm, sprinkled with cinnamon sugar.
Note: Strübli may also be prepared in a spicy version by leaving out the sugar and adding more salt to the batter. Top with caraway seeds and serve with an aperitif.

147

# Schlaatemer Rickli

*4 eggs, 150 g ($^3/_4$ C) sugar, 500 g (1 lb) flour, $^1/_2$ tsp
salt, 70 g (2$^1/_2$ oz) butter, 1 tsp grated lemon rind, 1$^1/_2$ dl
($^1/_2$ C) cream, fat for deep-frying, confectioners' sugar*

Beat the egg with the sugar until creamy. Combine the flour with the
salt and sift into the egg cream. Melt the butter, let cool a bit, then add
to the dough. Add the lemon rind and quickly stir the mixture into a
smooth dough. Form into a ball and cover with a cloth. Let stand overnight.
Roll out the dough 3-4 mm (approx. $^1/_{10}$ in). Cut it into 12 cm (5 in) and
fold these over into triangles. Let cool for half an hour, then fry in
180° C (356° F) deep for 3-4 minutes until golden brown. Place on
wax paper to cool, then sprinkle with confectioners' sugar.

# Schenkeli
# (Sweet Pastry)

*50 g (4 Tbs) butter, 130 g ($^1/_2$ C 3 Tbs) sugar, 2 eggs,
1 Tbs kirsch, 2 Tbs sour cream, 1 pinch salt, 1 tsp
grated lemon rind, 250-280 g (2$^1/_4$ C) flour, fat for
deep-frying*

Mix butter, sugar and eggs until foamy. Add kirsch, sour cream, salt
and lemon rind. Gradually sift in the flour. Stir until it forms a firm
dough. Chill overnight. Form finger sized rolls. Pinch both ends like
a cigar. Deep-fry at approx. 170° C (338° F) slowly until golden
brown. They must not brown too quickly, as they should be done all
the through. When done, they will easily pop open.
Note: One could also form the dough into little balls.

# Sweet Dumplings

*3 dl (1$^1/_4$ C) milk, 1 pinch salt, 100 g ($^1/_2$ C) sugar,
60 g (2 oz) fresh butter, 250 g (2 C) flour, 4 eggs, fat
for deep-frying, 3 Tbs sugar, 1 tsp cinnamon*

Bring to a boil the milk, salt, sugar and butter. Add the flour all at one time. Remove the pan from the stove and knead the mixture with a wooden spoon until you have a smooth dough. Let cool for a few minutes, then work in the eggs one by one until the dough is shiny. Let rest for 30 minutes.

Heat the fat. Drop balls of batter from a tablespoon and deep-fry in batches over medium heat until golden brown. Drain and place on paper towelling. Mix the rest of the sugar with the cinnamon and sprinkle over the dumplings. Serve hot.

## c) Sundries

### Cream Caramels

*750 g (3³/₄ C) sugar, 1 L (1 qt) cream, a bit of butter, oil*

Mix the sugar and cream. Cook, stirring constantly, until it turns brown and the mixture reaches the soft-ball stage. Pour onto a well buttered tin. Spread evenly and cut into squares until still warm using a knife dipped in a bit of oil.

Note: Instead of 1 L (1 qt) cream, you may use a half milk, half cream mixture; but the caramels will not be as soft as the ones made with pure cream.

## Roasted Almonds

These are sold primarily on the occasion of the traditional Fall Fair in many cities and towns.

*150 g (5 oz) almonds, 150 g (¾ C) sugar, oil*

Blanche the almonds, then pinch or rub off the skins. Pat dry with paper towelling. Place the almonds in a skillet and lightly brown without fat, turning them constantly. Cook the sugar and 2 Tbs water in a separate pan until the sugar is dissolved. Add the almonds. Stir for 5-10 minutes until the nuts are completely coated. Remove from heat and let cool. Return to heat until the sugar liquidifies again. At that moment, pour the nuts onto the greased (with oil) tin and separate with a fork. Let cool on the tin.

## Entlebucher Coffee

This is a sweet drink for cold days. The Swiss drink it with Lebkuchen, fruitbread, after dinner or after a day of skiing.

*5 dl (2 C) water, 2 tsp ground coffee, 1 small pine twig, lumps of sugar as desired, träsch (a schnaps made of fruit with a core, i. e. pears, apples)*

Add the coffee and the pine twig to the water and scald, set aside until the coffee powder settles. Fish out the twig. Place 2-3 lumps of sugar each in tall heat proof glasses. Pour in the coffee; it should be as thin as tea. Then add a generous amount of träsch or, if not available, a fruit schnaps of your choice.

# Notes and more recipes

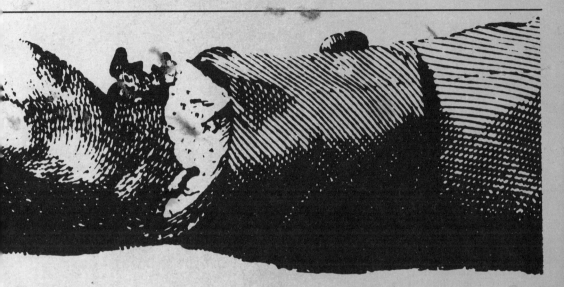

# Index

## Soups and Stews

## Fish

# Meat, Innards, Poultry and Game

## Spicy Pies and Pastries

## Desserts

## Cakes and Pies, Cookies

### a) Cakes and Pies

## Traditional Holiday and Deep-Fried Pastries, Sundries

# Comparative measures and weights

| Continental | American (approx.) |
| --- | --- |

## Liquid

| | |
| --- | --- |
| 1 Litre | 1 quart |
| 7½ dl | 3 cups (C) |
| 7 dl | 2¾ C |
| 6 dl | 2⅓ C |
| 5 dl | 2 C |
| 4 dl | 1½ C |
| 3½ dl | 1⅓ C |
| 3 dl | 1¼ C |
| 2½ dl | 1 C |
| 2 dl | ¾ C |
| 1½ dl | ½ C |
| 1 dl | ⅓ C |

## Weights

| | |
| --- | --- |
| 10 gram | ⅓rd oz − 1 Tbs |
| 20 gram | ⅔rd oz − 2 Tbs |
| 30 gram | 1 oz − 2½ Tbs |
| 50 gram | 2 oz − 4 Tbs |
| 100 gram | 3½ oz |
| 500 gram | 1 lb |

## Abbreviations

| | |
| --- | --- |
| L | Liter |
| C | Cup |
| qt | Quart |
| kg | Kilogram |
| g | Gram |
| lb | Pound |
| oz | Ounces |
| Tbs | Tablespoon |
| tsp | Teaspoon |

The recipes are for four servings, unless otherwise noted.